How to Change the Image of Your Church

John David Webb

Creative Leadership Series
Lyle E. Schaller, Editor

Abingdon Press / Nashville

HOW TO CHANGE THE IMAGE
OF YOUR CHURCH

Copyright © 1993 by Abingdon Press

This book is printed on recycled, acid-free paper.

Library of Congress Cataloging-in-Publication Data

WEBB, JOHN DAVID, 1943–
    How to change the image of your church/John David Webb.
    p.   cm.
    ISBN 0-687-11613-9 (pbk. : alk. paper)
    1. Church growth.   2. Communication—Religious aspects—Christianity.   3. Symbolism in communication.   I. Title.
    BV652.25.W433   1993
    254—dc20   92-31401

This book is dedicated to my family. First, it is a living tribute to those who have cared for me most. My wife, Judy, has endured through my two decades of graduate studies. My children, Leslee, Brad, and Michal, have sacrificed time and energy because of their dad's workaholic personality. My mother, Edith Webb-Slack, has been a constant admirer of all her children, encouraging us with her cheerfulness.

Finally, this book never would have happened without the support of my first and favorite mentor, the late John M. Webb, former Professor and Academic Dean of Lincoln Christian College in Illinois. His chief desires for his children were solid educational experiences and long, successful ministries in God's kingdom. I don't know that we've succeeded in those goals yet, but without exception, we are attempting to do the tasks, each in our own way.

"To God be the glory!"

Foreword

"We have a lot of first-time visitors, but few of them return a second Sunday," commented a veteran leader of a hundred-year-old, ex-rural congregation that was surrounded by farms being transformed into residential subdivisions and retail facilities. "What can we do to encourage more of those newcomers to join our church?"

"About twelve years ago, the first black families began to move into this neighborhood," reflected a longtime member of what had been founded in 1891 as a German Lutheran parish. "A couple of years later we called a new pastor, who came with a firm understanding that we would do everything within our power to become a racially integrated church. That decision cost us about thirty families, but those of us who have hung in here were determined to make it work. We were convinced that it was God's will for us to welcome all newcomers, regardless of color.

"I'm sorry to have to tell you it hasn't worked. During the past decade, our Sunday attendance has dropped from an average of 165 to 70, and we have fewer than two dozen black members. On a typical Sunday morning, we have about 45 women and 24 men. Nearly all the whites are past sixty, and most of the blacks are older women. What went wrong?"

"This community doubled in population between 1980 and 1990," explained the mayor of a suburban city to a mission-developer pastor. "The church my husband and I have been members of for nearly thirty years has dropped from an average attendance of nearly 500 to about 350.

"Directly across the street is another church that was founded more than a hundred years ago. We have a better building and more off-street parking, but their attendance has nearly doubled in about a dozen years, while ours has dropped.

"The lesson in that for a new minister is that population growth does not automatically produce church growth! In my opinion, this town already has enough churches. If you plan to start a new church here, you should know you've come into a highly competitive community."

The most useful frame of reference for diagnosing what happened in each of these three illustrations is not a church-growth perspective. The obvious common thread is the inability of three of these four congregations to be able to reach, welcome, serve, and assimilate new generations of people who do not share a common geographical heritage with the long-tenured members. That, however, does not provide any automatic explanations.

The simplest beginning point could be to examine the competence, dedication, relevance, productivity, and personality of each of the pastors. That could provide some clues, but it also might lead to scapegoating, which would overlook more systemic factors.

Perhaps the best frame of reference for analyzing what happened is communication theory. Through a combination of symbols, stories, names, symbol systems, and other components of its communication network, one of these four congregations was able to show newcomers that they really were welcome. We can begin to understand communication by reflecting on the power of symbols and names.

It is difficult to overestimate the impact of symbols and names on our lives. When we first meet a stranger, we know we will be more comfortable if we can learn the name of that stranger and that stranger will learn and remember our name. The importance of names can be seen in the effort new parents devote to selecting a name for that first baby, in the choice of a name for a new church, in the allocation of space on a tombstone in the cemetery, and in picking a name for the team that has just been awarded a major-league baseball franchise. The importance of names can be seen in the design of income-tax forms, drivers' licenses, and street signs. We depend on names to guide us through life.

As recently as the middle third of the twentieth century, most newcomers to a community, as they began to shop for a new church home, were guided first by the denominational names. Names give meaning to our journey through life.

Actually, this emphasis on names oversimplifies life. We rely on both names and symbols to guide us in making choices. Thus some of today's church shoppers automatically will choose one congregation while rejecting several others, simply because of the denominational name.

Other shoppers, however, will visit as many as a half-dozen or more congregations in their search for a new church home. Each one will be evaluated, not simply by the name, but also by many other criteria. One may impress the visitor as a dying church, while another conveys the image of a vital, lively, vigorous, challenging, and healthy parish. A third may seem solid, dependable, predictable—and dull.

In a fourth, a visit to the nursery informs the first-time visitors that this is *not* the place we will leave our precious first-born, eight-month-old baby. A Sunday morning visit to a fifth congregation may convince the church shopper that the pastor is more interested in paying the bills than in saving souls or preaching the gospel. It may be the sixth church on the list that persuades the first-time visitor, "This is the place for us!"

Each of these reactions was to a set of symbols that communicated messages about the essence of that parish. In many churches, the most influential symbol is the pastor. In others, it is the building. In at least a few, the most influential symbol is the congregational singing. In most, however, it is a far more complex combination of components. This book is an introduction to the power of communication patterns in congregational life.

In our best churches, the symbols are chosen deliberately in order to send the messages that the congregation wants people to receive, to respond to, and to remember. These are what Dr. Webb identifies as "enabled" churches. By contrast, many more congregations are "disabled" by a counterproductive communication system.

By combining the insights from communication research with on-site studies of several congregations, Professor Webb explains the differences between "enabled" and "disabled" churches. He also offers specific and detailed suggestions on how to become an enabled church.

This is a book for curious and creative leaders who are interested in using the best insights from communication research for enhancing the ministry of their worshiping community.

LYLE E. SCHALLER
Yokefellow Institute
Richmond, Indiana

Contents

Acknowledgments

In any study of this nature, there are more people to thank than can be mentioned. Besides my wife and my three patient children, many others have encouraged me. My very dependable advisor, Dr. James L. Golden, agreed to work with me even after his retirement from the faculty at The Ohio State University. And though neither knew me well, Dr. Paul Bowers and Dr. James Hikins served on my dissertation committee and offered excellent advice and help.

The people and ministers of many churches helped with their support and willingness to open their records and minds to my many questions. Most notable of these are Ben Merold and the Eastside Christian Church in Fullerton, California. They not only offered themselves, but provided financial aid for my travels to study other congregations.

I remember, too, the support and encouragement of the people of Martin Road Christian Church in Dublin, Ohio, during my years at Ohio State. They allowed me the time away to study and served as a testing ground for ideas that may have seemed strange to them.

I am also grateful to the congregations and their ministers studied in depth through this book: Leith Anderson and Wooddale Church in Eden Prairie, Minnesota; Darryl Bolen and First Christian Church in Greenville, Illinois; Tom Wolf and The Church on Brady in Los Angeles, California; Dave Johnson and Church of the Open Door in Crystal, Minnesota. Each provided abundantly of their time and energies to set me on the right course. Del Amo Christian Church in Torrance, California, was also extremely willing to allow me to examine its life.

Additionally, I received support from faculty members at Pacific Christian College. I am thankful to Dr. Gerald C. Tiffin, Academic Dean, who made my schedule workable during the time I was completing my dissertation and writing this book. I am equally thankful to Dr. Elwyn Buche, a sympathetic ear and a sound advisor. My older brother, Dr. Joseph Webb, contributed toward many of the insights through his writings and counsel.

Kathy Ganz Termeer, a former Billy Graham staff member, and Kay Heck, a professor at Pacific Christian College, spent hours proofing and editing both the dissertation and the manuscript. Judy Webb and Julia Staton proofed and offered helpful comments for clarity and precision. My dear friends Gordy and Judy Bryan opened their home and refrigerator during several trips to the Twin Cities. And last but certainly not least, Lyle E. Schaller took a chance that this book would meet the needs of thousands of congregations.

A work of this type is never the product of one person. I am deeply grateful for the many who have contributed in so many ways. Mentioned or unmentioned, they are a vital part of this book.

Preface

A marvelous image runs like a theme through the classic musical *Fiddler on the Roof*. It is Tevye at prayer. The bewildered father seeks so much to be the traditional, dominant father figure, but at the same time, he wants his wife and daughters to be free to choose their happiness. Alone, conversing with God, Tevye says, "On the one hand . . . ." Then he petitions, "But on the other hand, is it so bad . . . ?" He is caught in his personal paradox.

No one fully escapes these contradictions. And the church, poised at the end of the twentieth century, also is caught in a paradox. On the one hand, advertisements about books, journals, and seminars on church growth nearly overwhelm church mailboxes; Christian colleges and seminaries have added courses and programs that emphasize church growth; many consultants and consulting firms are focusing on church growth. We have more information than at any other time in the church's history.

On the other hand, the vast majority of churches in the United States are not growing at any significant rate. In fact, many churches are declining, and an alarming number are simply closing down. This phenomenon is not limited to a single geographical area or circumstance. In the major cities of our nation, one will find hundreds of church buildings that have been turned into community centers or warehouses.

On the south side of Columbus, Ohio, five or six congregations of the churches in my tradition follow a fairly typical pattern. In the 1920s and 30s, the largest congregation was South Church, which averaged well over 700 per Sunday. South had two services each Sunday morning—one for men and boys, the other for women and girls. That church no longer exists. Two miles down the road, Southwood was built. It continues to hold forth, but it is far smaller than it was in the 1940s and 50s.

Next came Benfield Church, another three miles along. Three miles farther south is South Side Church. Both are struggling congregations. Four miles farther on is Madison Church, a twelve-year-old congregation that experiences a solid rate of growth each year. Many members of this congregation had attended one or more of the other south-side churches and had moved after each had enjoyed its day in the sun. Of the five congregations, only one can actually be described as a "growing" church.

Rural congregations are not doing any better. During my college and seminary days, I pastored small churches in south and central Illinois. In many of those counties, typical of much of rural America, one-room churches were as common as one-room schools. Though the churches have been slower to die than the schools, many are now used for barns or have been left to deteriorate. The few remaining struggle on, held together by aging members who hope against hope that something might happen to turn them around. Though they once were vital and often a good training ground for young preachers, they have little chance for survival. Sadly, they are dying churches.

Perhaps the saddest of all are the new churches which, though located in rapidly growing suburban areas, have not made a significant impact on those burgeoning communities. While many do show numerical increases in membership, their growth does not match the population expansion. Even harder to explain are congregations in rapidly expanding communities which show no growth at all and, in extreme cases, cannot hold on to the numbers they once enjoyed. All these types of struggling congregations—the once thriving urban churches, the small rural churches, the slow-growing and nongrowing suburban churches—can be designated as *disabled congregations.*

The paradox of the nongrowing suburban congregations is that many of America's fastest-growing churches are located in similar areas. Congregations like Saddleback Valley Community Church and the Crystal Cathedral in Orange County, California, and Wooddale Church and Church of the Open Door in suburban Minneapolis, are in fast-growing communities.

So it is not location alone that makes churches grow. Congregations like The Church on Brady, in East Los Angeles, and First Christian Church in Greenville, Illinois, are growing churches in nongrowing, even declining areas. These congregations can be labeled *enabled congregations.* That term can even be applied to some congregations which, over time, should be dying but are maintaining themselves in a positive way, limiting declines to admirable percentages.

Another part of the paradox is that enabled congregations host "church-growth clinics" which explore their patterns and means of growth. The programs are well attended by pastors and lay leaders from disabled congregations, looking for help. Yet when these leaders return to their congregations armed with new ideas and programs, they do not enjoy the success of the enabled congregations.

These paradoxes raise a series of questions:

1. What are the differences between these divergent types of congregations?

2. Why are some enabled and others disabled?

3. Can a disabled congregation become an enabled congregation? If so, how?

Communication Study

This book presents a communication analysis of enabled congregations, to demonstrate that the answers to these questions are found in the *communication patterns* of the respective congregations. The terms *enabled* and *disabled* are drawn from communication research. Because positive communication is a vital element in enabled congregations, and because disabled congregations generally communicate negatively or poorly (both internally and externally), I have discovered that a focus on communication principles has great potential for local congregations.

The heart of the communication paradox is that, *though some congregations know church-growth principles and attempt to put them into practice, they create communication symbols and stories that lack the power to enable their ministry.* On the other hand, many churches that have little knowledge of church-growth principles have created enabling symbols and stories. In the middle of this paradox are congregations that do understand and use the church-growth principles effectively and have purposefully created enabling symbols and stories. This book will focus on these enabled churches.

In chapter 1 we will explore the key characteristics of disabled and enabled congregations. Chapters 2, 3, and 4 will consider three enabled congregations, their symbols, symbol systems, and communication stories. Chapters 5, 6, and 7 will show the reader "how to" do it. These chapters will demonstrate the practical way to discover a congregation's symbols and story, some steps that can help create more enabling symbols and continue the story, and a means of measuring the enabling or disabling patterns of a congregation.

The key data in this book are derived from models of enabled churches. The risk of using models is that some will attempt to duplicate the ideal without doing the work needed to understand how the model church became enabled. The reader is encouraged to study the examples carefully. But the real work will be in understanding how the enabling symbols developed in each congregation. Attempting to duplicate symbols might be helpful, but every congregation is unique; thus, its symbols and story will be exclusive to its own community. When readers do the hard work of creating their own unique symbols, those symbols will have enabling power.

Through disciplined work, prayerful study, and the guidance of the Holy Spirit, each church possesses the potential of becoming an enabled, growing body. My prayer is that each one will commit the time and energy—to the glory of God and the building up of Christ's body.

I

What Enabled Congregations Look Like

When it was founded in late 1959, Far West Fellowship* had all the signs of a congregation on the verge of "blowing the doors off." It consisted of a solid nucleus of Christians who had worshiped with another area congregation but had now moved into a rapidly growing suburb. Several well-respected leaders had been on the evangelistic team of their former congregation. Within a few weeks, they were able to secure the recreation building of a new community park between two major highways. They were also able to hire an experienced part-time minister.

Far West Fellowship's hopes were further raised by the relocation plans of another area congregation which had planned to establish a church in the same area. Merger talks united the two groups. The new relocation group brought nearly 60 members and, equally important, a considerable bank account. Since this congregation had recently sold their building, they were ready and willing to quickly invest in property and build their own building.

Far West Fellowship grew from 20 to 90 people in its first year. It was ready to buy land, build, and pay a full-time

*Not the real name of the church described here.

minister. It enjoyed experienced leaders, some of whom were committed evangelistic callers. The church's ideal future site was secured just three blocks from the new West High School, near a developing shopping area.

Growth came comfortably. Within five years, the congregation numbered more than 150; after seven years, 180. Between 1959 and 1968, however, growth in the community had swelled from 20,000 to more than 100,000. During those eight years the congregation completed two building programs. The members became a tightly knit group after doing much of the physical labor themselves. They quickly outgrew these new structures and began talking about a third.

After those years, a major setback occurred. The minister and his wife decided to divorce. He announced his resignation one year in advance. Because of this unusual circumstance and the minister's failure to negotiate an earlier departure, confidence in all leaders declined. As a result, attendance dropped to about 140.

In 1969, a new minister was called, growth began again, and by 1975, the congregation surpassed 210 in average attendance for several months. The congregation then hired a part-time youth minister and placed the minister's wife in a salaried position of music director. Much of the credit for growth was given to the establishment of the four choirs which she directed.

Because of this credit for growth, coupled with the fact that she was better educated and more experienced than the youth minister, the minister's wife believed that she deserved a salary greater than that of the youth minister. When she was not given a raise, she cut back her involvement by reducing the number of choirs. This reduction had a negative impact on the program and caused hard feelings among many within the congregation.

Three other situations also impacted the congregation. First, plans for a new sanctuary were ultimately rejected by the church board, and this became a source of contention among the leaders. Second, the minister became heavily involved in a local service club and the community sports program in which his children participated. Third, several leaders resisted growth because new families diluted their power bases. The presence of "outsiders" revived fears carried over from their former congregation. They appeared to believe the church and property might be overtaken by "strangers."

During 1975, the same year it reached its highest attendance, a move to fire the minister began. This effort produced secret meetings and a strong division between older and newer members. A motion to fire him failed, but with controversy now centered around both the minister and his wife, a downturn began which would mark the congregation for the next fifteen years. What had once been a "shining star" of its tradition was now a declining congregation.

By the time the minister resigned, nearly fifteen years later, the congregation had dwindled to less than 70. The neighborhood also had changed ethnically, and the church's ability to impact the neighborhood now appears limited, though some slight growth has taken place since the arrival of a new pastor in 1990. The church continues to operate on a shoestring budget, has few short- or long-range plans, and possesses a low self-esteem. From all appearances, it would be classified as a "disabled congregation."

How does one recognize a disabled church? The most obvious sign rests in the numbers. But that is not always an accurate indicator. Though numerical growth may be *the* obvious sign, some enabled congregations exist which, because of location and declining population, either hold their own or decline only slightly. Some disabled congregations may be growing, but their rate of growth is completely disproportionate to community development. Numbers are not a sufficient indicator.

This chapter will present some basic characteristics of disabled congregations and some key principles for discerning enabled congregations. These descriptions provide a basis for answering the question, "Is the congregation I know best enabled or disabled?" Before considering the qualities of enabled congregations, it will be helpful to look at some characteristics of disabled congregations.

Characteristics of a Disabled Congregation

Many church-growth books give a clear picture of what disabled congregations look like. The following characteristics are the most commonly seen in nongrowing congregations.

1. Though congregations should be aware of and see the importance of their history, disabled congregations often *spend a disproportionate amount of time talking about the past.* Such comments as "we remember when . . ." and "the good old days when . . ." are commonplace.

2. The congregation *appears to have a low self-esteem,* often crippled by an *attitude of hopelessness and/or helplessness.* It is a very contagious disease which spreads through the body quickly.

3. The congregation *attempts to grow without goals or objectives.* The members have not learned the significance of a clearly defined mission (purpose) statement or short- and long-range planning.

4. Although some congregations do set goals and establish plans—often very excellent plans—they *establish an unrealistic time frame.* The results hoped for in six months are often 18 to 24 months away. As a result, they decide that the plan, not the timetable, was the problem.

5. Further, in planning and goal setting, disabled congregations *rarely anticipate the possible consequences of a specific course of action or program.* An unexpected fallout leaves them suspicious of trying anything else new.

6. *Members of the congregation have grown older.* The average age increases yearly, and though some younger families remain, the small number of children makes program variety difficult. There is much talk about gaining younger families.

7. Like the overall membership, *the leaders are older and have served for many years.* They often are not willing to take risks or accept new ways of doing things; they do not adjust readily to change.

8. Disabled congregations *often face recurring financial problems.* Programs are often shortchanged or delayed by limited resources.

9. Disabled congregations *frequently focus inward rather than outward.* Survival and maintenance of current standards overshadow outreach. Problems are blamed on forces outside the church.

10. Disabled congregations normally *lack a sense of urgency.* They generate little energy to accomplish tasks.

11. Disabled congregations *often profess to be protecting the "truth" when they are most likely protecting their turf.*

12. Disabled congregations *often communicate a fear of the unknown.* "What if" questions are generally perceived as negative rather than positive.

13. Disabled congregations *talk about people leaving rather than being added.*

14. *Buildings and grounds* of disabled congregations *often are in a bad state of repair.* Funds for maintenance are insufficient.

15. Though many congregations would not accept criticism from the outside and would dismiss comments about a lack of unity, *discord often marks the internal workings of a disabled congregation.* Meetings are often filled with turmoil and dissension.

16. Disabled congregations *have difficulty managing visitors.* Some do not pay enough attention to their guests. No one assists visitors or offers directions. Conversely, some

congregations overwhelm visitors by paying too much attention to them.

17. Disabled congregations *are unwilling to change.* They refuse to adopt new programs for fear of losing people, but fail to recognize that people leave because things are "stale."

18. Disabled congregations *often make changes at the surface level only.* Changes are copied from others without examining any rationale for doing so. When no results follow, they can easily explain their return to the more comfortable ways.

19. *The minister of a disabled congregation often conveys the impression that this is just another job, is visibly bored* with the situation, and/or *is looking forward to relocating or retirement.*

20. Many disabled congregations believe that *they must remove the current minister and find a successful "superstar" to ignite a flame.*

These characteristics, summarized from a variety of church-growth books and organizational communication studies, are not exhaustive. The reader might easily say, "You could have included this or that." The attributes do, however, represent major factors that often are readily apparent and provide a good starting point from which to look at a congregation the reader knows best. An honest evaluation is critical. One or two of these characteristics might be easily overcome, but if several are involved, the congregation probably has very serious problems.

How to Read This Book

As noted earlier, it is a paradox of our time that more material than ever is available on church growth, even when a vast majority of churches are not growing. This book intends to approach the positive implications of enabled congregations and the problem of disabled congregations from a communication standpoint. It will not focus on programmatic issues as such, even though various approaches will be examined; it will highlight the types of communication practices which "enable" congregations. It will suggest that a congregation is generally either enabled or disabled by the symbols, symbol systems, and communication story it expresses to its members and potential members. If readers are looking for a "quick fix" or some "magic beans" that grow instantly, this book will fail to fulfill their expectations. The suggestions made will demand hard work at a high cost.

Church-growth researchers stress the need for good communication, and this book is written from the perspective of a communication researcher who has added church-growth studies for better understanding. Thus, here church-growth principles will be controlled through communication standards. The different starting points will become obvious.

Readers will become familiar with communication terms such as *symbol*—a common word, but one possessing a specific definition in communication studies. *Symbol* has been variously defined; it has sometimes been used as a synonym of *word*. In this book, it will be used in a wider context; almost anything can become a symbol in the church.

Other key terms will be *symbol systems* and *communication story*. Like *symbol*, these phrases have been variously defined and used by different authors. Readers should not be overwhelmed or confused, since these terms will be carefully defined as you read the chapters. The terms *disabled* and *enabled* have already been introduced.

Some readers will be sensitive to persons with physical or mental conditions which create opportunities and challenges that others do not encounter. Our society often marginalizes or ignores persons who live with such challenges. Readers will be given a fuller understanding as they continue.

Concepts about disabled churches have already been

introduced; it is now time to shift attention to the major theme of this study: enabled congregations.

Principles of the Enabled Congregation

The following principles are drawn from several theorists, including M. E. Pacanowsky, N. O'Donnell-Trujillo, E. Bormann, L. Putnam, F. Jablin, and my own research.

Principle 1

All organizations, including churches, possess their own unique symbols, symbol systems, and communication stories. Enabled churches manifest corporate (congregational) symbols, symbol systems, and stories which coincide with the individual and family symbols, symbol systems, and stories of a majority of their potential population.

Principle 2

An enabled congregation has a clearly defined mission statement and clearly established goals, from which its level of accomplishment can be measured. No organization or congregation can be enabled without knowing what it wants to accomplish and the means by which it can arrive at the task.

Principle 3

An enabled congregation communicates the message that it widely distributes power and opportunity. All persons wishing to participate will be given the occasion to do so.

Principle 4

An enabling organization maintains open and decentralized communication. Whereas many organizations (churches notwithstanding) communicate in a "top down" style, enabled organizations broaden the base of communication to allow as many persons as possible into the mainstream of thought. They discover that open communication allows greater creativity and acceptance.

Principle 5

An enabled congregation will use "integrative problem solving," in which the problems of the organization are placed in the hands of those most likely to understand the problems and most committed to their solution. "Task forces" of those directly involved will be the most productive problem solvers.

Principle 6

An enabled congregation allows "challenge" in an atmosphere of trust. Trust is bilateral; ministers and church leaders who ask for the trust of the congregation must willingly allow challenges to their decisions and trust the congregation's judgment.

Principle 7

An enabled congregation provides appropriate rewards and recognition, as a means of encouraging better performance and more responsibility on the part of the total membership.

Churches Need Help

Churches are dying. They have become disabled by their own inadequacies. They have produced verbal and nonverbal symbols which cause them to "shoot themselves in both feet." This does not need to be. Though they are fewer in number, there are many enabled congregations. These congregations have created interesting and attractive symbols which relate to their potential audiences.

This chapter has introduced the two basic sets of characteristics. The traits which disable a church are numerous. Twenty were listed, although readers will be able to suggest others. This chapter has also listed key principles of the enabled congregation. Others would suggest additional premises, and individual congregations will add to both lists. Though disabled congregations will be used for comparison, the remainder of the book focuses on the enabled congregation.

The next three chapters will discuss the basic communication principles found in growing congregations. By studying these enabled congregations, readers will see the importance of having strong and enabling symbols, symbol systems, and communication story.

Let me introduce a church with enabling symbols: Wooddale Church of Eden Prairie, Minnesota.

II

Enabling Symbols

The Crystal Cathedral
Hollywood Presbyterian Church
The Church of the Open Door
The Vineyard
Wooddale Church

The descriptions that congregations use are important. Their names tell the world who they are and what they are about. In many cases, mainline denominational names are key. In other cases, denominational designations are avoided, and a name that reflects an idea is selected. Those who name the group determine the impact of this primary symbol. Names—symbols—affect the persons who are attending for the first time. But the name is not the only symbol chosen. For further identification, a slogan is often chosen:

"The church in the know and on the grow"
"A busy church . . . always serving"
"The Community Church of Orange County"
"A Place to Belong—A Place to Become"

Both a name and a slogan are designed to represent the perception of who and what a congregation is. Besides the external names and descriptions, internal symbols also are labeled: choirs, youth programs, women's groups, men's prayer breakfasts, fellowship nights, the annual bean supper, and so on. Such descriptions become synonymous with, and particular to, individual churches. Conversations about churches are filled with what communication literature calls *symbols*. The compilation of the many symbols produces what becomes a *symbol system* and *communication story*. Symbols, symbol systems, and the communication story are the means of communication.

In this chapter, the uniqueness of symbols will be studied. Symbols identify an individual or a group. More than that, they *enable* corporate (congregational) structures. Though corporate symbols usually are created by a small number of individuals, they gain effectiveness as they spread throughout an organization. The size of the unit is not critical. This chapter will show how symbols are created and give meaning to a congregation.

Wooddale Church, Eden Prairie, Minnesota

Wooddale Baptist Church, a Baptist General Conference congregation, was opened in the Minneapolis suburb of Richfield in the early 1940s. From the beginning, it could be described as an enabled congregation. Within the first decade, it surpassed the 500 mark in average attendance, and during the 1950s and 1960s, the congregation continued to grow with the community. After thirty years and several major building programs, the congregation enjoyed a building that seated in excess of 750 worshipers, had sufficient educational space, a gym/multipurpose room, and office space for a staff of fifteen. Utilizing multiple services, the congregation maximized its available space.

The congregation's property, however, had only fourteen parking places. In spite of repeated efforts to provide more parking, the congregation's efforts were thwarted. The church's offer to build a multilevel parking garage on the library property across the street was rejected by the city as "impractical" and "expensive to maintain." As a result, the church attempted to purchase several houses on their block, but two property owners refused to sell at any price and successfully blocked efforts to raze other houses for parking. Though the congregation had averaged over 1,000 per Sunday for about seven years, it seemed blocked from additional growth by the limited parking area.

In the late 1970s, Leith Anderson was called to the pastorate. Supported by the lay leaders and staff, Anderson led the congregation to a vision of renewed growth which included a relocation to a suburb nine miles away. Primary in the vision was the congregational mission statement. Anderson described its creation:

> Wooddale Church in Eden Prairie, Minnesota, states that "the purpose of Wooddale Church is to honor God by bringing lives into harmony with Him and one another through fellowship, discipleship, and evangelism." To fulfill its mission, the church's organization is comprised of a Fellowship Board, a Discipleship Board, and an Evangelism Board. In the case of Wooddale Church, it was not a matter of drafting a new purpose statement, but of studying the existing statement, revising it somewhat, and then having it broadly owned by the congregation. (*Dying for Change* [Bethany Press, 1991], p. 163)

The relocation was supported primarily by showing that the mission statement could not be fulfilled in Richfield.

By the early 1980s, the elders were convinced that the move would be necessary to reestablish Wooddale's growth and advancement. In their discussions, they created symbols of growth through relocation. Then slowly and progressively, they introduced members to the relocation symbols. As the circle of committed individuals increased, the reality of moving improved. Three years later, the congregation fully accepted the new symbols and voted to re-locate.

From 1984 until 1990, the congregation worshiped in temporary quarters on its new property as construction progressed. In November 1990, the congregation met in its new Worship Center for the first time. Although other phases were under construction, the worship center gave Wooddale the symbol of a permanent home.

It would be naive to think that such a great transformation did not cause some major disruptions in the life of the congregation. However, in spite of the upset, worship attendance passed the 2,000 mark during the transition. One of the major reasons for this growth rested in *carefully selected symbols,* which enabled Wooddale to make this move a positive advancement.

Creation of the Symbol

In the beginning was the object, and the object was with the symbol, and the symbol was the object. And whatever Adam named it, that became its designation. Naming is an important function in life. It begins communication, but it does much more than that. It is the very means by which life and reality are linked together. Until an object or idea is named, it possesses little value.

From the earliest days of their lives, children are taught to name objects. "Mama" or "Dada" are more than the first words parents want children to speak. They are the source of identity which finally allows the parents to accept the roles they have created for themselves. The symbols, in this case the words "Mama" or "Dada," provide a relationship to the object named. Thus, reality is tied to the symbol. The child perceives the adult as "Mama" and connects the symbol and reality. The woman accepts this symbolic link and says, "Yes, that is who I am." The husband, who usually had referred to this woman as "wife" may soon symbolically describe her as "mother of my children." For many, a given name is changed to a relational name, and beyond: "Mary" changes to "Mother" or "Honey" becomes "your father," as roles change. Naming is an extremely significant activity. Over time, we learn objects by hearing a name, a symbolic representation for them. Figure 1 illustrates what happens in the naming process.

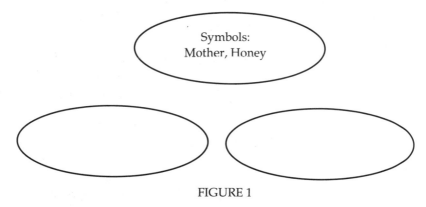

FIGURE 1

Perhaps the best remembered of all symbol creations is the story of Helen Keller. Anne Sullivan, her teacher of many years, carefully documented the discovery of Helen's learning. It began on that day during her seventh year when she discovered the name for "water."

> This morning, while she was washing, she wanted to know the name for water. . . . I spelled w-a-t-e-r and thought no more about it until after breakfast. Then it occurred to me that with the help of this new word I might succeed in straightening out the mug-milk difficulty. . . . We went into the pump-house and I made Helen hold her mug under the pump while I pumped. As the cold water gushed forth, filling the mug, I spelled w-a-t-e-r in Helen's free hand. The word coming so close upon the sensation of cold water rushing over her hands seemed to startle her. She dropped

the mug and stood as one transfixed. A new light came into her face. She spelled "water" several times. Then she dropped on the ground and asked for its name, and pointed to the pump and the trellis, and suddenly turning around she asked for my name. I spelled "teacher." Just then the nurse brought Helen's little sister into the pump-house and Helen spelled "baby" and pointed to the nurse. All the way back to the house, she was highly excited, and learned the name of every object she touched, so that in a few hours she had added thirty new words to her vocabulary. (Helen Keller, *The Story of My Life* [New York: Double-day, 1903])

Over the course of the next few days, Helen Keller searched for new symbols—names—for everything within her reach. Her world was being expanded by the addition of new symbols.

Created and Attached Symbols

The definition of a symbol can range from relatively simple to highly complex, but simple definitions are usually best. *Symbol* is defined as *anything to which a name has been applied and meaning attached.* Further, a symbol produces feelings and emotions. One of the most accepted principles of communication suggests that all messages contain both content (meaning) impact and relational (feelings) impact. Communication—especially oral communication—seldom takes place without both parts of the message impacting the hearer. Words are the most common of our symbol forms, but there are many others.

Students regularly use *pen* and *paper* in the *classroom.* Each of these four words is a symbol. Pen and paper are normally used for note taking. But if the teacher asks students to "take out a pen and paper," the symbol may change from "note taking" to "test." Consequently, the identity of and the feelings about these simple instruments are altered.

In the eighth grade, I experienced those feelings in a shattering way. I had always been a decent math student, but during my first week in a new school, I failed my first math exam and was assigned to the group known as the "slow train," a negative symbol. I was frustrated for the entire year, often becoming physically ill on exam days. The symbols "math test" and "slow train" still stir deep emotions in me.

One should not be surprised when potential church members have negative reactions to such symbols as "church" and "sermon." After all, these words may carry feelings of "boredom," "punishment," "requirement." The mere mention of "churchy" symbols evokes fears and anxieties as real as my experience in math class. Though a symbol is simply *an expression used to describe something by assigning it a name and attaching meaning to it,* it cannot be taken lightly. Symbols are powerful because they carry both descriptive and emotional impact.

There are many other types of symbols. *Music*—sounds of different pitches arranged in an appropriate fashion become a musical symbol. Though few know it as "Suicide Is Painless," television viewers identify specific symbols as the theme from "M*A*S*H." We also recognize the sounds associated with "Cheers" or the theme from *Gone with the Wind.* Music becomes a part of the symbol system of an individual or a group.

Self is another important symbol. There has been much discussion about positive and negative self-images. Over time, all persons create a symbol system by which they are identified, both to themselves and to those with whom they interact. Personally, to one individual, I am "husband"; to three, I am "father"; to one group, I am "pastor"; to another, "professor." I recently received a letter from a friend who jokingly addressed it to "Reverend, Doctor, Professor John D. Webb." Congregations are a blend of symbols which produce their self-image. Congregational self-images are just as vital as individual self-images.

Places can be symbols. Persons distinguish their homes by the way they are decorated, such as Early American, Country, or Southwestern. Church buildings and Sunday school classrooms are symbolic of the Christian world. Churches that have moved an existing church-school class from "its" room may have found the well-being of the class and the congregation threatened.

I once worked with a congregation in which the senior women had changed their classroom into a library and reading room. They had paid for bookshelves, comfortable chairs, and appropriate decorations. When it was suggested that this particular room was too large for their class and that a larger class needed to exchange rooms with them, most threatened to leave the congregation rather than move. Needless to say, their library remained their Sunday schoolroom.

Objects become symbols. Congregations often consider artifacts as "holy," as if based in a higher authority. For example, one congregation would not permit any part of its communion table and pulpit furniture to be rearranged. Even though it was often difficult to work around those bulky items during weddings or children's programs, no alternative was allowed. When this congregation remodeled its sanctuary and moved those "holy" articles, some members left the church.

Colors are effective nonverbal symbols: "_____ green" or "_____ blue" are often linked to "Army green" and "baby blue." Others might tie the colors to khaki, or emerald, green or sky blue. Colors affect moods and influence decisions. Houses with red carpet tend to sell better than those with blue floor coverings. When we combine the images of place, objects, and colors, we can explain why some people are attracted to a certain church building itself. Many who find the Crystal Cathedral's stark glass-and-steel image unattractive would love a simple white-clapboard building. On the other hand, the simple building would turn others away as being too old-fashioned.

Dress also is symbolic. Controversy often arises over the way a minister or church leader dresses. We say, "She looks like an executive," or "He must be a firefighter." Our tradition does not use clerical garb; a minister once preached about "ministers who wear dresses" to show his dislike for robes. Visitors may not return because of the way people dress; the person accustomed to wearing a dress or a suit and tie could easily reject a congregation where people arrived in shorts and casual attire. Dress can make a difference to some people.

The ability to communicate and produce understanding is based in sharing known symbols. The word *communicate* literally means "to hold in common"; thus our ability to communicate is based on our ability to share like symbols and symbol systems. It is the naming of objects, ideas, feelings, or events differently which creates confusion. Unfortunately, many things block shared understanding. For example, if I say, "The hammer is broken," a carpenter will envision his favorite nail-driving tool, while a concert pianist might picture an instrument with an unplayable key. *Symbols must be shared to reduce confusion.*

Importance of Congregational Symbols

Organizations, like individuals, are involved in naming. They develop symbols which clearly identify them and/or their products. For organizations, almost *anything* can become a symbol. Religious organizations formulate definite symbols. For example, most churches suggest that "people" comprise the church. But like the world, they have structured themselves toward "church" as a "building" and use it accordingly. "We should all go to church" is not an accurate reference to *church*, if, in fact, one were talking about the membership and not a building. Yet the word is so ingrained in our religious symbols that most fail to distinguish between the people and the meeting place.

Symbols also identify specific Christian groups. The root of *denomination* is *name*. Thus, members are not only Christians, but Lutherans, Methodists, Baptists, Congregationalists, Mennonites, and so on. My tradition distinguishes itself as a "brotherhood"—a term deplored by those sensitive to gender language—while at the same time, it balks at any suggestion that it is a "denomination." Further, certain symbols identify a particular denomination. If you are a Friend, you worship in the "meetinghouse." If you are a significant lay leader in the Baptist Church, you are a "deacon." The parallel office in the Presbyterian Church is an "elder." We all once recognized nuns by their black and white habits. *And individual congregations develop their own symbols.* That will become very clear as we look at Wooddale Church.

Wooddale's Relocation Symbols

Though Wooddale communicated enabling symbols through most of its first thirty years, the 1980s proved to be the most intense time of symbol study and advancement. Anderson and the Wooddale elders determined that the move from Richfield to Eden Prairie would be positive and growth-producing. Their efforts took place on several levels. Internally, the relocation vision evolved through the creation of a series of intermediate symbols.

The initial symbols were finalized by the elders after several months' work. Once completed, these were shared with the congregational opinion leaders; the second level to be informed were the staff and members of the church boards. Some symbols were modified during this process, as will be seen in the next few paragraphs.

The third group included Sunday school teachers, growth group leaders, youth leaders, choirs, and other active members not in leadership roles at that particular time. These members shared the modified symbols with a new audience, and the symbols were again revised by those hearing the vision for the first time. Ultimately, all interested church members shared in the vision through congregational meetings.

At each level of presentation, some members rejected the symbols. In many cases, people left Wooddale for congregations where the symbols were more suited to their particular beliefs, values, or attitudes. Some who rejected the relocation symbols stayed because of connections to other symbols valued enough to overcome the uncomfortable relocation symbols.

Externally, Wooddale's leaders began a careful study of the Eden Prairie community, determined to create symbols in keeping with the community symbols. They intentionally set out to relate to their new neighborhood. Doctrinal truths would not change; they were non-negotiables. But through the community surveys, personal interviews, and a marketing firm's research, the congregation established symbols for reaching Eden Prairie.

Other Symbols

Relocation and building programs were not the only symbols that comprised this portion of the Wooddale story. In fact, after the completion of the first phase of buildings and the physical move, relocation symbols became unnecessary and building programs secondary. Overall, the congregation created many enabling symbols.

1. Wooddale Church

One of the key elements included in the relocation was dropping the symbol "Baptist." Although upsetting to many long-time members, research concluded that the symbol possessed a negative connotation and needed to be removed.

2. Purpose Statement

The mission statement of the church continues to be a key symbol for many Wooddale members. It particularly drives congregational leadership (see Leith Anderson's statement on page 33).

3. Motto

"A Place to Belong. A Place to Become." Based on the findings of the research team which surveyed the Eden Prairie community, this motto reflects the idea that Eden Prairie was composed of newcomers looking for a place to put down roots and join with others for "fellowship and support."

4. Logo

For the last six or seven years the congregation had used a nondescript logo which had little significance, only leading people to ask, "What is it?" After the completion of the Worship Center, the present logo displays the church's eighty-foot steeple atop a portion of its complex, providing an immediate visual focus of the property. It towers above most commercial buildings in the area and quickly identifies Wooddale Church.

5. Pastor

Even before leading the congregation through this change, Pastor Leith Anderson's name had become synonymous with the church. It is "Leith Anderson's church," and he is "Wooddale's pastor." The designation of "pastor" is highly significant to the majority of the members. He represents the congregation's paid and lay leadership, and though he is not physically present for every service or meeting, his presence pervades every function. Other staff members are well-known by function, yet are considered simply a part of the Anderson symbol.

6. The Wooddale Campus

The thirty acres currently owned by the congregation comprise the most visible representation of the congregation. On the campus are several key locations, including the "Worship Center," the "Great Room," the "Child Care Center," the "Woods," and the parking lots. The Worship Center, for example, is key because it is the focal point for "Celebration." It houses the pulpit, the majestic pipe organ, the baptistery, and the other symbols of practical theology. Further, it is used for public gatherings; it is one of the homes of the St. Paul Chamber Orchestra. Though no other room possesses the power of this symbol, each fulfills its purpose.

7. "Celebration" focuses on worship and praise.

Celebration is the chief reason for building the worship center. It intentionally points the worshiper toward God. Congregational singing and other music are designed as praise. "FaithStory" focuses on the way God is at work in the lives of members. Anderson's preaching is the focal point of celebration as he shares his faith and life; it is the ultimate act of worship for Wooddale.

A key element in the celebration is the traditional worship format. At a time when many congregations have chosen a more informal style, featuring praise choruses and Scripture songs, Wooddale has maintained the more traditional approach.

8. "Congregations" are the many smaller groups which meet for study and fellowship, similar to Sunday school classes in other congregations.

They are led by trained members of the congregation and follow a regular course of study. Each is designated by its several symbols, which include the class name and the leader. Congregational symbols include names such as "Cornerstone Congregation." Congregations range in size from about 25 to 100 persons.

9. "Cells" are another level of support and fellowship.

Composed of 10 to 15 persons, these groups meet at various times in members' homes for study and support. Leaders are required to attend weekly preparation sessions.

10. "Support groups" of all types are provided.

The regular list of weekly and monthly meetings includes groups for singles, the recently divorced, persons who have lost loved ones, alcoholics and others with dependency needs, and a host of others.

11. "Boards"

Although they are less visible and not as well-known, the various boards of the congregation represent the leadership and visionaries of the congregation. Currently the boards carry the symbols "Board of Elders," "Discipleship Board," "Evangelism Board," "Trustee Board," and "Fellowship

Board." Each board has well-defined responsibilities and is headed by an elder.

12. The weekly newsletter, *The Wooddale Witness*, carries news of the congregation to members and regular attenders.

13. "FaithStory" gives members the privilege of telling their pilgrimage.

Each Sunday morning, a member of the congregation shares personal testimony with the congregation. The symbol was modified from "Witness Stand" at the time of the move to the new worship center.

14. "Septemberfaire" is the annual opening of the church's year, a time when the community is made aware of Wooddale with some type of publicity delivered door-to-door.

The many activities resemble what one might find at a community swap-meet or art fair. There are games for children, food stands, adult activities, as well as places where the various programs of Wooddale are explained.

Many other lesser-known symbols are used by various groups within the congregation. Youth programs, choirs, and outreach ministries—all are given special designations by which they can be easily identified. Though they are important symbols, they remain subordinate to the broader symbols. Wooddale has been very deliberate in choosing symbols which have appeal to current and potential members. Active members become as familiar with the congregational symbols as they are with personal and family symbols.

Individuals and organizations create symbols which provide the means by which they are known both internally and externally. Symbols are both verbal and nonverbal pieces of information about an organization. In the case of a congregation, symbols will include the name of the congregation, its building and properties, its minister(s), its programs, the names it selects for different parts of its work, as well as the way it presents itself to its various audiences. These symbols will create the means by which people determine their affiliation with the church.

This chapter has focused on Wooddale Church, an enabled congregation which intentionally has created symbols that give it vitality and produce growth. The symbols developed during its first few years emerged in a somewhat haphazard manner. It was noted, however, that during the last decade, Wooddale has expressly evaluated its symbols.

First, the congregation measured what the members were saying internally. Concepts like the name—"Wooddale"—the "Cells," "Congregations," "Celebration," and an unchanging theology have made Wooddale secure even through the chaos of its relocation.

Second, it was observed that Wooddale intentionally analyzed its new community, selecting appealing and appropriate symbols. These findings allowed the church to create images that would be inviting to Eden Prairie families. The most visible change was the dropping of "Baptist." The installation of a pipe organ demonstrated its appeal to a traditional audience. At a time when congregations were moving toward informal worship, Wooddale discovered that Eden Prairie preferred traditional hymns, choirs, and the pipe organ. Consequently, it opted for these symbols.

As this study moves ahead, we will look at a second phase of this communication theory. From the collection of its symbols, a congregation builds its *symbol system*. The next step studies a different church in a different community, to see how symbols mesh into systems, to provide a well-recognized picture of the congregation.

III

Enabling Symbol Systems

"Let me tell you about our church. You've probably seen it; it's out near the high school. You can't miss it if you ever go to a football game. We're right behind the ballfield. It's the large yellow-brick building with the cross and steeple on top.

"We have a wonderful youth program and a great choir. Our preacher is young and exciting. His sermons are always inspiring, and he's really friendly. And you'll love our new building. It's really a great place to worship. And your wife will love the Bible study and the aerobics classes. You really ought to visit First Presbyterian!"

Contained in these two paragraphs are symbols that describe a local congregation. When various symbols, such as "yellow-brick building," "friendly preacher," "cross and steeple" are linked together, they create the second level of communication, the "symbol system."

Symbol systems are created when individual symbols combine into a settled and predictable pattern. Individuals create their personal symbol systems from symbols that have personal significance. Families select from their members' symbols to create family symbol systems. Special family functions and special names given to family members—"Pumpkin" or "the Caboose"—combine into family symbol systems.

Every organization creates its unique symbol systems. In churches, symbols such as congregational names, ministerial staff names, building descriptions and dedications, words that designate special groups or programs, and so on, link into congregational symbol systems. These are a result of a congregation's attempt to identify itself, not only for its own members, but for external audiences. In fact, congregational symbols and symbol systems become a part of new members' initiation. Accepting and sharing these symbols with others provide a key for knowing that the new members are now a part of the church. Symbol systems comprise a vital link in a congregation's communication.

First Christian Church, Greenville, Illinois

Greenville, Illinois, a typical midwestern village, is located about forty miles northeast of St. Louis along Interstate 70. Greenville is the seat of Bond County, primarily a farming area with a population of 15,000, a decline of 1,000 in the past twenty years. While some people drive the 40-plus miles to the St. Louis area, most are employed locally. The largest employer is Greenville College, a Free Methodist coeducational school with about 800 students enrolled. Carlyle Rubber Roofing and United Stationery, the next-largest employers, have fewer than 150 persons on their payrolls. Greenville is a lower-middle-class city, with nearly 25 percent of its population over 60 years of age. Staunchly conservative, Bond County is "dry" and no pornography is sold legally. With a population increase from 4,600 to 5,000 in twenty years (1970 to 1990), it is obvious that church growth in Greenville does not result from urban sprawl.

First Christian Church was founded in 1877 and has been one of Greenville's two strongest churches since the 1930s. The congregation originally worshiped in a structure designed to seat about 250 persons. The building then included a sanctuary, basement classrooms, and church offices, but had limited parking and little property for expansion. When attendance reached 400 in the early 1960s, it was obvious that First Christian had outgrown its aging facility, so the leadership proposed to relocate. The new building also would provide off-street parking and easy accessibility for older members.

After the new building was completed, several members remained at the original structure, forming Greenville Christian Church. That church has experienced little growth, and though the attendance of relocated First Christian dipped briefly as a result of this defection, it soon experienced renewed growth.

First Christian has been marked by three long pastorates. Pastors R. T. Hickerson (in the 1930s and 40s) and Frank Bush (in the 1950s and 60s) served for about twenty years each. Four years after he was called as youth minister in 1973, Darryl Bolen was elevated to senior minister. Attendance between 1973 and 1977 increased from 328 to 341, but since 1977, growth has been steady: in 1980, it reached 407; it surpassed 500 in 1984 and 600 in 1988. Bolen projected that it would surpass 700 during 1991. While the community's population grew less than 500 after the church's relocation, First Christian has enjoyed a net increase of nearly 350 persons in active membership.

During these years of growth, the congregation established its symbols and symbol system. Before looking at First's symbol system, let us consider the way symbol systems are built.

Building the Symbol System

From the beginning, an organization creates its symbols. Soon thereafter, these symbols are linked together to produce unique and distinct meanings. The union of these symbols creates the symbol systems, *a combination of individual symbols which provides the communication by which we link to our internal world and to the external world around us.* Though *words* are the most common symbols and the foundation for all symbol systems, they do not often stand alone.

Symbol systems are both verbal and nonverbal. Though a symbol can stand alone, symbol systems combine verbal with other verbal and nonverbal images. The statement, "Get out of this room," can be expressed both verbally and nonverbally. One can communicate the message by uttering the words or by making a physical gesture, pointing to the person and then to the door. When coupled with an angry look, the symbols send a clear message. Combine the words and motions, and the message is even stronger. There are many possible combinations that can produce symbol systems.

Messages can be confusing when verbal and nonverbal symbols are contradictory. "I believe you" can be expressed verbally, but can be invalidated nonverbally with a doubting facial expression. "We are a friendly congregation" is the most restated set of contradictory symbols uttered by the church. The words and the actions that follow the words send differing and conflicting messages. Figure 2 illustrates the progression from symbol to symbol system.

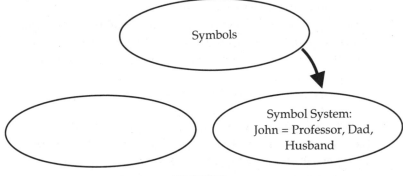

Symbols

Symbol System:
John = Professor, Dad, Husband

FIGURE 2

Building the Organizational Symbol System

Words arranged in a poetic fashion and placed with an appropriate set of musical notes can transform individual symbols into dramatic symbol systems. In the gripping musical *Les Miserables*, musicians transform the simple words "one day more" from a bland phrase into a powerful, stirring song which leaves most of the audience profoundly moved or in tears. When the costumes, makeup, scenery, and interactions are blended, the music becomes a highly moving expression of each character's personal dreams.

If we see what we identify as a college or university campus, we are usually curious about its name. The same is true of a church building. And we sometimes associate the name of the minister with the name of the congregation. Thus one might say, "This is Leith Anderson's church," and expect the hearer to know that one is speaking of Wooddale. Linking two or more symbols creates a symbol system.

The Crystal Cathedral and Robert Schuller are well known around the country and the world, as well as in Southern California. But in the total symbol system of that congregation, one would find that the symbol "Crystal Cathedral" represents the full campus which includes several other buildings, the "Hour of Power" television ministry, the "Glory of Christmas" musical, and a host of other images. Yet all those separate symbols create the symbol system of the Crystal Cathedral, and even of Robert Schuller. Every organization produces many clearly distinguishable symbol systems. All congregations create and maintain symbols and symbol systems which clearly identify them and make them distinctive. First Christian Church has a clearly established unique symbol system.

Symbols of First Christian Church

The symbols of this church grew out of a natural course of events. Unlike Wooddale, which hired a marketing firm to help identify and create attractive symbols, this congregation developed its own symbols somewhat randomly, as most churches do. In spite of this unsystematic approach, these symbols have proved to be attractive to a significant number of people. The community seems to be the catalyst for First's continued growth. The key symbols of First include:

1. First Christian Church of Greenville—The name has been constant from the beginning.

2. The church building—It has moved through about five or six stages of development since its relocation. Although it includes a large area, it has not, like Wooddale, been depicted as a "campus."

3. Darryl Bolen—The current pastor stands in a long heritage of well-respected ministers.

4. Hospital visitation—This is a key element of the outreach and identification of First Christian Church.

5. *The Greenville Christian*—The weekly newsletter contains "Bolen's Alley" and other symbols centered on personal names.

6. Family nights—These are the focus of the fall and spring programs.

7. The Fall Sunday School Kickoff—Each September begins with a challenge for a large attendance and the annual potluck dinner.

8. Sunday afternoon basketball league and Body and Soul—sports provide activities for adult members.

9. Special slogans for special events:
   "All Ears Night"—a corn roast held during the summer when corn is available.
   "Every Member in Church," "You're Something Special," "We Can Do It," and "Come Alive in Christ"

have served as annual themes, although a theme is not selected every year.

"Miracle Offering Day" was created in 1988 as a means of raising $70,000 for the remodeling of the sanctuary.

Like Wooddale, names have been attached to Sunday school classes and other smaller groups. These are important, but not as distinctive as those that describe the entire congregation. Many of the symbols are linked together in the thinking of many FCC members; these comprise the symbol systems of the congregation.

First Christian's Symbol System

Five distinct symbol systems are shared by the Greenville congregation:

1. The symbol system links names and persons.

The most obvious linkage are the names "First Christian Church" and "Darryl Bolen." Officially named First Christian Church, the congregation is also known as "Bolen's church," even when this connection is denied. This is especially true among individuals who are more familiar with Bolen than with the church as a whole. Community leaders and non-members visited in the hospital do not hesitate to refer to the church in this way.

Conversely, Bolen is First Church's man; his identity in the community is linked predominantly with the church. If he ever left the congregation and remained in the community, he would be forced to establish a new identity. "Bolen" and "First Christian Church" are bonded; each draws identity from the other.

Other names are linked into this symbol system as well. Externally, these include "Church on Killarney," "church near the high school," and "the church that comes to see you while you're in the hospital." Internally, First refers to itself as a "family church," a "growing church," or a "Bible-believing church."

2. The building symbol system reflects the growth that has taken place since the 1960s.

Because of the numerical growth, building additions and their symbols have enjoyed a life of their own—particularly, the auditorium. Growth can be measured in large part by three expansions of the worship center. This was also one of the first congregations of its tradition to have a gym/multi-purpose area. Among congregations in a small community, it was a church ahead of its time.

Further, a special one-time program called "Miracle Sunday" focused on building expansion. It caused people to see the connection between building expansion and increased numbers. It allowed them to symbolize themselves as a growing congregation.

3. The staff symbol system revolves around the minister.

First Christian is proud that several ministers have spent a major portion of their calling here. Bolen has become a highly respected minister, like his predecessors R. T. Hickerson and Frank Bush. Greenville's reputation for long ministerial service is well known among churches of its tradition, as well as in the local community.

Staff identity revolves around Bolen. Though the church secretary has been at the church longer than Bolen, she is now identified with Bolen's team. Associate ministers are considered an extension of Bolen; even lay leaders stand under the Bolen umbrella. Though official documents would dictate against it, the congregation has created and sustained Bolen's persona as key to this symbol system.

4. The outreach symbol system linked several symbols.

Internally, the *Greenville Christian* informs members about programs, activities, and other news items. Its counterpart is the Sunday bulletin. Externally, the hospital visitations serve to identify the congregation to patients and their families. Evangelistic visitation follows a newcomer's first-time attendance. Care programs and other church activities provide identification with the community. The goal of this external symbol system is to show that First Christian cares about the people of the community; the goal of the internal symbols is to show that it cares about its members.

5. Programmatic symbols also link into a system.

As noted above, programs like family nights, men's basketball, and women's aerobics are important parts of this symbol system. Events like the "Fall Sunday School Kickoff" and "All Ears Night" occur annually and bind the congregation together. The special names of classes and other groups also fit into the programmatic symbol system.

Symbol systems are vital links between members of the congregation. Though each member and nonmember do not have an attachment to every symbol system, the systems provide a means by which all connect to some aspect of the church. It is not vital that individuals attach to every, or even the same, symbol system(s); however, it is necessary for members to share some symbols and symbol systems in order to remain connected to the congregation and sense that they "belong."

Comparison of Enabling and Disabling Symbol Systems

Two congregations comprised the original study of symbol systems: We will call them Eastside Church and Far

West Church. Because the congregations were of the same tradition, there were many similarities:

1. They were part of a group that called itself the Restoration Movement.

2. They had roots in conservative, midwestern traditions.

3. Paid leaders were referred to as "ministers" and refused to be called "reverend"; these leaders were trained in the tradition's colleges and seminaries.

4. Lay leaders were known as elders and deacons.

5. Both believed that church ordinances are baptism by immersion and weekly Communion.

6. Both supported missionaries directly, rather than through a missionary society.

7. Each linked the minister's name with the congregational name.

Here the similarities stop. The symbols and symbol systems produced both enabling and disabling effects. Several are obvious.

1. Congregational Name and Ministerial Identity

Like the Greenville Church, Eastside loved her minister and the people gladly referred to it as "Ben's church." They dreaded the thought of his leaving as he approached retirement age. He was proud to represent the congregation at national events; he made tapes on church growth, explaining how Eastside had expanded.

On the other hand, as Far West began its decline, its members often went out of their way to separate themselves from their minister. He was made the scapegoat of anything negative. They seemed to be waiting for him to leave, so that someone new could be hired. Though symbolically linked, the congregations held opposite attitudes toward their ministers and about their own self-identity.

2. Descriptions of Size and Effectiveness

Eastside possessed a symbol system around success. These included highly charged symbols of "growth," "expansion," "activity," "busy," "serving," "mission-minded," "innovative," "risk-takers," and "a congregation to be imitated." The members published their accomplishments widely. They talked of continued growth and advancement.

Unlike Eastside's positive symbols, Far West used symbols of diminishing size, such as "declining," "struggling," "departure," "uncaring," and "unconcerned." It was not unusual to hear about "the way it used to be" and "remember when."

These symbol systems played into either the enabling or the disabling self-identity, which pushed the congregations in opposite directions.

Created Realities Which Enable
and/or Disable

Eastside and Far West give an idea of the way symbols and symbol systems affect a congregation's outcome in terms of growth or decline. The creation of symbols and symbol systems begins with some actual events and happenings within the church. Building programs, changes of members, changes of ministers, community growth or decline, and membership increases or decreases are typical of events which could produce symbols. From its own observations of these realities, a congregation creates its unique view of itself and assigns appropriate symbols by which to identify and clarify the realities. The congregation's own description of reality produces an idea about itself which eventually becomes more real than the actual event. These new symbols become the created reality in the symbol system (see Figure 3).

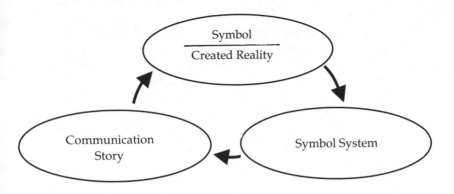

FIGURE 3

Borrowing from an old cliche, one could say, "As a congregation thinketh in its mind, so is it." Eastside's story demonstrated this. Sensing its success, Eastside created strong evangelism programs and participated in many attendance contests which led to good growth early in its life. All these programs and contests were given creative names (symbols). Mottos about growth, such as "Bring a friend to Eastside," appeared regularly. When Eastside saw itself as a growing congregation, its leaders produced the symbol systems that depicted growth. Even during a period of retrenchment caused by a decline in the local economy, the symbols of growth were maintained. Believing that they would continue to grow, Eastside maintained the growth pattern for three generations.

Far West Church was begun by whites who were fleeing an ethnic invasion. Members of one congregation had already moved to a growing white suburb and were meeting in a neighborhood park building. They were soon joined by many members of another congregation which had sold its property and were relocating as a whole. The newly formed group talked of "evangelism" and "growth," but symbols were created to protect itself from outsiders. A small group which preserved the existing social order wanted to evangelize people "just like us," which produced a fortress symbol system.

Significant growth would put this protective mentality at great risk, so when growth began and evangelism brought in young people and families who were "different," those in the fortress resisted. As the obstinate members rallied around their fortress symbols, those who were new were gradually forced out. Today they are still protecting their imagined fortress. The first "fortress" group has been replaced by another, an official church group which accommodates many of the same people.

Once the perceived reality produces a created reality, the "created reality" becomes more significant than the reality itself. The perception of and belief about an event becomes more dominant that the actual event. Growth allowed Eastside to create and sustain enabling symbols. Conversely, the fortress mentality became deeply ingrained in Far West's created reality. Its withdrawal into itself created and sustained maintenance symbols.

A congregation which views itself as growing may continue growth symbols even during decline. Conversely, congregations which perceive themselves as "stagnant" or "dying" sustain those symbols, even if they are experiencing a period of growth. Often the overall effect is that a congregation will return to its perceived reality because it believes that this is its destiny. Symbols and symbol systems are powerful influences on churches and become self-fulfilling prophecies.

In this chapter, the discussion focused on the movement from symbols to symbol systems. It was noted that churches, as well as people and organizations, link symbols to create symbol systems. Symbol systems provide a second method of both internal and external communication.

It was also noted that churches produce symbols and symbol systems based on certain realities observed by and about the congregation. The interpretation of these realities becomes the created reality—the heart and soul of what is believed about the organization. However, it is possible for the "created" realities to be misleading. Congregations which perceive themselves as very friendly because the members all like one another are often viewed as unfriendly by outsiders. Believing they are friendly, they are unmoved when told they are not. They have created a false reality. Symbol systems that stress the "good old days," "the need to get some new life and blood," and "get back to where we were" suggest potential weaknesses which may be hidden in the created reality of "we're okay the way we are." Whether accurate or false, the created reality and the reality become intertwined and inseparable.

Symbols and symbol systems become either enabling or disabling. Whether positive or negative, symbol systems can grow so ingrained that they are almost impossible to change. As long as they are positive (enabling), it is generally beneficial; if they are negative (disabling), they are most likely destructive. Wooddale, First Christian, and Eastside produced enabling symbol systems which, in turn, created positive realities; as a result, growth came because the congregations believed they could grow. Their symbol systems vitalized the growth. However, Far West is typical of many disabled congregations which fail to comprehend the disabling message of their own symbol systems.

In the next chapter, the final piece from communication theory is added. As The Church on Brady in Los Angeles, California, is examined, we will discover how symbols and symbol systems combine to produce the communication story of a congregation, which further either enables or disables that congregation.

IV

The Enabling Communication Story

Lake Wobegon, Minnesota: "Where all the women are strong, all the men are good-looking, and all the children are above average."

For nearly fifteen years, Garrison Keillor kept America abreast of the little town that rested between Lake Wobegon and Adams Hill. "It's been a quiet week in Lake Wobegon, my hometown" captivated the attention of millions of radio buffs waiting to hear the latest news. Although located in the center of Minnesota, Wobegon was lost in the junctures of the map.

The Communication Story of Lake Wobegon

Lake Wobegon has several landmarks: Ralph's (pretty good) Grocery, where "If we don't have it, you don't need it"; the Sidetrack Tap, where the men gather to drink a Wendy's and swap stories; the Chatterbox Cafe, featuring the town's food staple—tuna hotdish; Lake Wobegon High School, home of the mighty Leonards; the Sons of Knute Lodge, regular meeting place of the Norwegian Bachelor Farmers; and Lake Wobegon, the spring-fed lake that empties into the Wobegon River before becoming a part of the Sauk River and, finally, the Mississippi.

Lake Wobegon has three churches. Lake Wobegon Lutheran Church is led by Pastor Ingqvist, a man of sufficient talents, but as a preacher, he does not measure up to the pastor of the Turquoise Tabernacle in Anaheim. There are several significant things about Lake Wobegon Lutherans. Their Norwegian background suggests they must have strong coffee with cream. Coffee is a staple of their diet and part of every Lutheran event. Important days of the year include Confirmation Sunday, marking the teens' rite of passage into church membership. All the Lutherans drive Fords purchased at Bunsen Motors.

Our Lady of Perpetual Responsibility Catholic was led for forty-four years by Father Emil. Though Keillor claimed ignorance of Catholic practices, he was highly interested in their ways. He was intrigued by such special days as the Feast Day of St. Francis, when the animals were gathered on the church lawn for their annual blessing. All the Catholics drive Chevys bought at the Main Garage.

Keillor's family belonged to the Sanctified Brethren, a small sect of true believers described by a young Keillor as Prostestants because "he didn't want to get into what they really were." A highly spiritual people, they possessed no building and partook weekly of the Lord's Supper as they worshiped in Aunt Flo's home. Sanctified Brethren argued over whether one can worship with other SB's who are in error. They are suspicious of Catholics and Lutherans with their unusual ways of worship. Like Lutherans, they drive Fords.

Keillor created a world of symbols and symbol systems to tell the story of his mythical town in Mist County, Minnesota. One quickly becomes immersed in the saga of Lake Wobegon and often begins to relate to the images of his or her own people and places. Suddenly, Lake Wobegon becomes Emden, Illinois; New Harmony, Indiana; or Bunn, North Carolina. It is real because one recognizes oneself in Keillor's little world. People hear their own real stories in Keillor's fictional story.

Every town, every organization, every church, has a story to tell. Some churches' stories are very positive and picture healthy, enabled congregations. Symbols of growth, new buildings, or growing missions programs abound. On the other hand, some congregations talk about the "good old days"; still others are extremely bleak, filled with complaints, pessimism, and despair. Both these latter types quickly discourage the listener; they can completely disable any congregation.

The repeated account of the organization is called the *communication story*. It expresses the congregation's self-perception. Like an individual's self-image, organizational stories pack a great deal of influence into what happens to a church. Stories are built from the congregation's symbols and symbol systems. Whereas symbols are the components, and symbols systems link components into units, the communication story relates the church's past from the beginning to the present moment.

It relates the congregation's created idea of itself and is handed down from one generation to the next; it is never completed. It is filled with inside stories and jokes, congregational secrets and deeds, and major themes developed over the years. Composed of interrelated symbols and symbol systems, the communication story comes in both compressed and expanded versions, to picture what the congregation believes about itself. The communication story is a crucial part of a congregation's created reality.

The Church on Brady, Los Angeles, California

Although the property of The Church on Brady (affectionately called "Brady") stands within sight and sound of the glamorous sections of Southern California, it reflects little showiness. Brady Avenue in East Los Angeles is just twenty blocks from Garfield High School, home of the critically acclaimed movie *Stand and Deliver*. East LA has been changing for more than five decades. When Brady began in the

1940s, the area and congregation were predominantly white. During the 1960s, the population shifted until it was largely Hispanic. Today Brady ministers to an urban cultural mosaic composed primarily of Anglos, Asians, and Hispanics.

Physically, the Church on Brady is surrounded by small, ordinary houses with yards often littered with junk cars, small stores with bars on the windows, people on the street waiting for the next group of day laborers to be hired, and severe poverty. Several families may occupy one small home, and two or more houses are often squeezed onto one narrow lot.

The congregation was founded in 1943 and first met in the Carpenter's Union building. The current location was purchased and occupied in 1948. During the ministry of John Ashcraft in the 1950s, the congregation grew to a membership and attendance surpassing 300. After Ashcraft's departure, the church began a steady decline. The few people who remained at the end of the 1960s were midwestern and southern transplants who commuted from distant suburbs.

Tom Wolf was in his mid-twenties when he accepted the call to First Southern Baptist. He arrived in July 1969 with the understanding that this was a seven-to-ten-year commitment, although he intended to stay at least twenty years. Against the wishes of the congregation, Wolf and his family moved into East LA. To establish his presence, Wolf walked the streets within a mile radius of Brady. For the first three years, there was little growth in the church; new memberships were offset by departures.

During Wolf's third year, the church began a decade of significant growth. Though the congregation was becoming predominantly Hispanic with a blend of Anglos and Asians, English-speaking worship was established as the common ground. Worshipers from all backgrounds desired this link to their Christian experience.

By the end of Wolf's first decade, the congregation had grown from about 70 to nearly 500. As a result, the congregation was being constrained by its limited property. Though Brady's attendance stayed around the 500 mark during the 1980s, its growth became channeled into other areas. Limited by its space, Brady looked outside itself. From 1980 through 1990, Brady was instrumental in starting sixteen new congregations—six in the Los Angeles basin and ten in other nations. In addition, a Spanish-speaking congregation of 300 grew in Brady's building before finding its own space.

Those years also found Brady consumed by a five-year building project. In spite of the many construction problems and cost overruns, Brady members found great satisfaction in building (literally with their own hands) and financing a $1.6 million building, when economically such a task seemed impossible. Since the completion of the building, Brady has seen renewed on-site growth. Average attendance is now over 550, and this growth continues even as Brady sends out many of its best leaders as international church planters. Unlike congregations in the suburbs with large facilities and expansive campuses, Brady has organized to fulfill its unique mission on very limited acreage.

But Brady is an exception. In an area where most denominations have given up or simply died out, Brady not only has stayed, but has become a beacon to the community and the world. Like Greenville, East Los Angeles is not where one would expect to find a growing, exciting ministry. Yet people from around the world come to learn from a congregation of amazing vitality.

Building the Organizational Story

When we discussed symbols and symbol systems, it was noted that though based in "reality," they produce a "created reality"—that is, they give expression to this perceived reality. After the symbols and symbol systems are well-established, organizations create what we will call the organizational story: *that combination of symbols, verbal and nonverbal, which become the symbol system; the continued use of the symbol systems produces the story of the organization* (see Figure 4).

However, that story relates a congregation's created reality. Like Keillor's Lake Wobegon, it contains both the real and the imagined. All organizations, including churches, have a way of interpreting reality to suit their needs. The communication story is shared among older members and passed down through new people. It comes in answer to a statement such as, "Tell us about your church." It establishes the meaning of the congregation's existence.

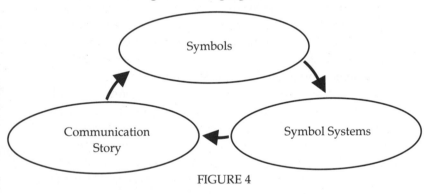

FIGURE 4

Organizations usually have overlapping and mixed symbol systems built into their stories. At Far West Church, for example, people shared stories about the "good old days" when the building was full, people were excited, and there was great hope for the future. One would believe that this reminiscing involved one single time in the church's life. However, upon delving deeper into the symbols being shared, it would be discovered that two different time periods were being recounted.

One member recalled a time during the tenure of the first minister when the building was full and the congregation progressing. Another member focused on the days of the second minister, when the same expansion was repeated. The first member never cared for the second minister, so even though the records clearly showed that the second growth spurt actually produced higher numbers than the first, that member's story overlooked the later time of success and growth. The second person, converted during the later period, recalled a story with similar symbols. However, that member was not even aware of the first minister's best days. The two members used identical symbols and shared the same story, but from two separate time frames. In communication theory, this is commonly called a representative anecdote.

Church realities include such things as the construction of new buildings, the coming and going of ministers, periods of growth, leveling off, decline, new growth, and so on. Getting to the actual incidents is important; they set the stage for a congregation's created story. Yet even though distorted, enlivened, short-circuited, or modified to make things look better or worse than they might have been, the story presents what the congregation truly believes about itself.

Like a quilt, a congregation's story is made up of many pieces of information which gradually form the whole of the blanket over time. The symbols are progressively shaped and reshaped. Historical realities certainly are not lost in the telling, but are intermixed through differing time periods and meanings. Yet the story recounts a highly accurate picture of the congregation's history. Variations of the story will exist; there will be disputes over the nature of events, conflicting dates argued, but the story gives the congregation its self-identity when passed on to succeeding generations.

One last factor must be pointed out. The congregational story has the power to generate new realities and symbols within the congregation. The communication story, as long as it is positive, energizes and enables a congregation. Conversely, if the story turns negative, it can disable the congregation. Figure 5 shows the circular nature of this process.

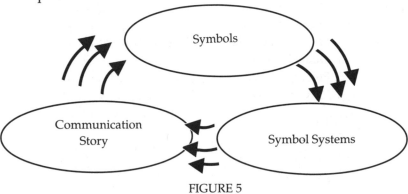

FIGURE 5

Symbols of Brady

It is Brady's story that will illustrate the enabling power of congregational narrative. Before the story of Brady is written, it would be helpful to consider the major symbols and the system into which they fit. The following outline shows the symbol systems as points, while the symbols within the system are shown as subpoints.

A. Names
  1. Brady or The Church on Brady
  2. Brother Tom
  3. International Urban Institute

B. Mission Statement: "The purpose of the Church on Brady is to become a spiritual reference point east of

downtown Los Angeles and a sending base to the ends of the earth."
   1. Spare Not Conference
   2. Church planters

C. Oikos Evangelism
   1. "The front door of your home is the side door to the church."
   2. Discovery Groups
   3. Lay Evangelistic Group Studies (LEGS)
   4. Oikos Bridges
   5. Persons of Peace
   6. Prayer Triplets

D. The Three C's
   1. Cells
   2. Continuation
   3. Celebration

E. Ministries
   1. Clean and Sober
   2. The Center for Community Counseling

It is from these key symbols and symbol systems that the Brady story builds.

Brady's Communication Story

On a sunny spring afternoon after I had been investigating Brady for several weeks, I might have asked a long-time Brady member, "Tell me about your church." If she were a typical member, this might be how she would have told the Brady story.

I'd love to tell you about our church! The Church on Brady began its life as the First Southern Baptist

Church. We were started by midwestern and southern settlers with Southern Baptist roots who were working in the California oil fields and defense industries.

As the community changed from Anglo to a multicultural mix (currently the congregation is 65% Hispanic, 20% Anglo, 15% Asian, African-American, and others), Catholics who were afraid of being tied to the name *Baptist* simply referred to us as "that little church on Brady." Finally, in 1977, we officially changed our name. Though we have retained our ties to the Southern Baptist Convention, the new name has removed a barrier to those who aren't Baptist. "Brady" is one of the best-known names in the area.

As long as the area was Anglo, the church grew. However, as the community changed, so did the church. After growing to 300 in the 1950s, we began to slip as Anglos moved out and Hispanics and Asians bought into the area. We were sustained by people who drove back in from the suburbs, and we went through eight pastors in ten years.

Brother Tom made the difference. He was pretty young when he and Linda (his wife) came. He made some people pretty unhappy when he announced that he would live within the Brady area. After twenty years, he still lives here. Brother Tom announced that he would stay at least seven years. And he not only stayed but brought a new evangelistic zeal to the church. Not everything worked, but he really has made a difference.

The whole Church on Brady reestablished an evangelistic zeal. We wrote a mission statement which stated that we were a "spiritual reference point east of downtown LA and a sending base to the ends of the earth." We wanted to reach some of the eight and a half million people who live in Los Angeles. Brother Tom led us to create Oikos Evangelism. *Oikos* is the Greek word for "household." We want it to be as well known as the Greek word *Agape*. Oikos is composed of a person's four different worlds: the family, the neighborhood, the work place, and friends. These are the places where evangelism can take place. We attempt to reach people on their turf.

We create our "Discovery Groups" in offices, in our schools, in our homes, and anyplace else where people can study the Bible. We don't have time to tell you all about it, but it really works. Stick around, and you'll learn all about "Oikos Bridges," and the "Person of Peace," and "Prayer Triplets." We have special classes where you can learn about all of these important concepts.

We're also concerned about world evangelism at Brady. It is not enough to just reach our immediate neighbors; we believe in planting churches around the world. In fact, we have begun ten churches in Mexico, the Philippines, and other places, as well as the six churches we've started here in Los Angeles. This summer we have teams working in Huntington Park and Cudahy. Every summer—and, well, all year round—we have young missionary recruits who come to Brady to learn about our methods and train in the trenches of Los Angeles. After all, there are more international people in LA than in any other part of the United States.

Missionaries from around the world come here for relaxation. Did we tell you about the "Spare Not Conference on World Evangelism"? Every fall, the congregation hosts a conference to promote church planting around the world. Last year's conference was called

"Carry the Light," and several hundred people came. We also have the "International Urban Institute" at Brady. It is associated with Grand Canyon University in Phoenix and offers master's degrees in urban education and in teaching English as a second language.

What about our own people? That's a good question. It seems that all the talk has been about others. Our people are sustained by our three C's. Our own evangelism is done through our *cells*, small home groups designed to reach our personal oikos. Most groups meet in members' homes, although some meet in schools, and our children share in their groups on Sunday morning. All our groups are required to reach new people. We build around the idea that "the front door of our home is the side door to the church." Groups that don't grow are rolled into other groups.

Then we also have *continuation*, the second C; we call it our Discipleship Training Institute. It meets on Wednesday evening and focuses on four types of studies: message, mission, ministry, and maturity. On Sundays, we join for the third C, *celebration*, a blend of joyous praise, and preaching from the Bible. Brother Tom applies the Bible text to everyday life. It is in celebration that all the cells are brought together for fellowship and praise.

There is so much that goes on at Brady, I know I've missed something, but as you get to know us better, others will fill in the voids.

Although much more could be said about this enabled church, it is possible to condense organizational story by highlighting one or two key components which present the essential nature of a congregation.

Having learned the symbols of Wooddale and reviewed the symbols and symbol system of First Christian Church in Greenville, it might be helpful to see their communication stories stated in a condensed version.

Communication Story of Wooddale Church

The story of the Wooddale Church can be summed up as the *intentional effort to mesh community and church symbols into a harmonious pattern.* The key word here is *intentional.* Through months of study, using both church personnel and a seasoned market analyst, Wooddale developed congregational symbols which blended with the symbols of Eden Prairie. More than any other congregation studied, these symbols arose purposefully. Whether it was the name of the congregation, the design of the building, the motto, logo, or worship and music style, the symbols were created and sustained with the community in mind. Wooddale has been avant-garde in its desire to draw its community with verbal and nonverbal symbols.

Although certain symbols were intentionally created at Wooddale, it must be clearly understood that the congregation's symbol selection has not altered its doctrines. Outwardly, the wineskins were chosen so they would not be disabling, while the wine of the gospel is as rich and full as ever. In preaching and teaching, Anderson and Wooddale made no compromise. Scriptural exposition and application have not been sacrificed. Wooddale is intentional in every facet of its program, so people can be reached with the power of its gospel message.

Communication Story of First Christian Church

The heart of First Christian Church's communication story suggests a "growing congregation meeting the needs of a nongrowing community." This self-image has allowed it to move from a good congregation, serving about 300 people in its community, to one that truly believes it is destined to continue growing. It has not attempted to grow through campaigns and slogans, but by a reputation of helping the people in the community and county. Nowhere is this more evident that in its hospital ministry.

First Church has now become large enough that its regular programming attracts families that desire a variety of activities for all their members. The growth of the congregation has also provided a sense of responsibility to continue the progress. It believes it can easily reach the 1,000 mark in this decade. Though that would not move it into the range of a "megachurch," it will remain a dynamic force in its community and a witness to what hard work can accomplish. Bolen and the congregation continue to preach the basic truths that the congregation has held for more than one hundred years.

Would a close scrutiny of this church's symbols and the development of a carefully designed symbol system produce gain beyond its current efforts? One cannot say. What is obvious, however, is that First Christian Church in Greenville, Illinois, possesses an enabling symbol system by knowing and meeting the needs of its community.

The realities and created realities of a congregation produce symbols, symbol systems, and, ultimately, the communication story. The story passes the created history from one group to another. The story has the power to produce new realities which, in turn, construct new symbols in a circular pattern.

All the examples—Brady, Wooddale, and First Christian—assist a congregation's understanding of why it needs to be aware of what the symbols and the story suggest. The symbols represent who and what the church is and help it to understand whether these messages enable it for growth or disable it for stagnation and deterioration.

The symbols and story are important, not so much as fancy ideas, but in evaluating whether it is reaping the harvest the Lord desires.

It is now time to turn attention to the critical task of discovering whether congregations are enabling or disabling themselves with their symbols, symbols systems, and story. Eastside Christian Church was the first congregation with which I tested these theories.

In learning how the characteristics of enabling or disabling are present in a congregation, you will be stepping into my shoes—you will become a communication researcher for your own particular church. As you are exposed to the basic steps of how to uncover the symbols, symbol systems, and communication story, be prepared to put what you have learned into practice. The welfare and future of your congregation may depend upon what you do with the information. It should go without saying that this changes you from a casual observer to a prime mover in your church's future.

V

Discovering Enabling
Symbols and Story

Eastside Christian Church, Fullerton, California

Eastside Church has enjoyed almost thirty years of continuous growth. Beginning with a group of some 100 persons, it has steadily grown to a membership of 4,500, with a regular average attendance of nearly 2,500 per week. Only twice in its history has it watched attendance averages drop below those of the year before. The first decline came early.

After five years of steady growth, the church reached a milestone by completing its first building project. The completion followed three difficult years, including a time-consuming search for available property in a booming market, the purchase of a vineyard in central California so that a land switch could be arranged, and the painful days of building. Slowly but surely, the land was purchased, plans completed, financing arranged, and ground broken. Eastside was about to move into a new building.

But a major setback came during the rainy season when the building was ready but the parking lot incomplete. Rain prevented paving for almost seven months; for many weeks, the congregation was unable to meet in the newly completed structure. Having already abandoned its rented space, Eastside was forced to meet in temporary facilities, and even after a rather awkward boardwalk gave access to the new building, it was highly inconvenient. By the time the parking lot was completed, some members and potential members had left and did not return.

Ministerial problems also arose during this difficult time. By the time the founding pastor tendered his resignation and left, the congregation had declined by several percentage points, the debt load was heavy, and the congregation was more discouraged, even with a beautiful, spacious new building.

The call of Ben Merold to the pastorate triggered a rapid turnaround. Old attendance records were surpassed; within three years, the size of the congregation had doubled. Eastside was one of several congregations experiencing significant growth in the north Orange County area; within the next fifteen years, the congregation enjoyed nearly a 1,000 percent increase over its 1968 average. It was one of the fastest growing churches of its tradition nationally and of any denomination in Southern California. Eastside was blessed by being in a rapidly growing community near a busy expressway and a major university.

The second decline came in 1977. This problem did not originate internally, but externally. Three decades of growth in Southern California had been tied to the aerospace industry, and a sudden severe decline in that industry negatively affected the whole region, including the churches. In less than a year, Eastside lost 400 members who were forced to move from the area because of job changes. This decline lasted only a few months, however, and by 1979, the congregation was growing again.

By the mid-1980s, however, that growth had slowed significantly. Though new people joined regularly, a similar number were leaving. By 1986 and 1987, the members were regularly asking themselves two questions: Why has growth slowed? What can be done to get things back on track?

Personal Involvement

Though I had not been invited to make a study of the congregation as a means of answering these questions, I came to Eastside in 1988 as a doctoral candidate with a desire to study communication issues in a growing congregation. Eastside was chosen because of its well-deserved reputation as a growing congregation, and because my current teaching position was at a college less than two miles from Eastside's building. It was coincidental that the congregation was attempting at that time to discover why its growth had slowed. The opportunity to study this congregation came at a very appropriate time for both of us.

As I began the Eastside study, I established a two-part, five-step plan which was presented and approved by the congregation's leadership. It was agreed that I would have access to all records, would find members encouraged to visit with me openly, and would be permitted to work directly with the staff as requested. This chapter is a brief description of the five steps I followed during the discovering of the symbols, symbol systems, and communication story of Eastside Church. This simple plan has been followed in other studies of both growing and declining congregations. It can provide the basics for discovering a congregation's communication story for those who are willing to make the effort.

Part A. Gathering Information

Step 1—Document Search

The first step will require a search for various types of materials. For example, at Eastside, I linked two distinct sources, which can be described as internal and external documents.

At Eastside, I began by reading nearly thirty years worth of *church newsletters*. This allowed me to discover key events and time periods in the church's history. It gave a general picture of the growth of the congregation, with regular reports of Sunday attendance, building programs, special programs, staff additions, and regular commentary by the senior minister.

Then I moved to other types of reading—*annual reports, meeting minutes, Sunday bulletins,* and *sermon outlines.* These documents often added specific details and explanations of what was happening in the church. One might find *congregational histories, appeal letters, information letters to members only,* and other written documents. At another church I studied, church papers were not available, so that search began with the abundant notes of church council meetings. You should begin with the most comprehensive church records you can find.

While searching congregational documents, *newspapers* and other *external records about the church, denomination, and community* are helpful. These will also provide help in understanding the local congregation. Research into the histories of Fullerton and Orange County allowed me to discover the parallel growth of the community and the church. It also showed that the population increase in Fullerton stopped in the early 1980s. This research also led to the discovery of a decline in the number of school-aged children and a slowly changing ethnic mix in the area. It was becoming clear that the resource pool of people was declining. Through such research, I learned that one of the other congregations studied was greatly influenced by an ethnically changing neighborhood. Because of this discovery, I conceptualized the "fortress mentality" which helped explain the congregation's inward focus.

Further, an *overview of the denomination's history* is helpful. These histories and records are often available from *district, state, or national assemblies,* or the tradition's *college libraries.* I discovered that Eastside began through a separation from Fullerton's First Christian Church by members who had become distressed by the changing organizational and theological position of their tradition.

The goal of the search is to uncover a congregation's symbols, symbol systems, and communication story. The initial study should focus on *key events,* such as *ministerial changes, attendance swings, community growth,* and *employment patterns*—anything that might affect the congregation positively or negatively. Nothing should be avoided or dismissed; a seemingly insignificant piece of information may open doors. I discovered that changes in the aerospace industry affected most Southern California congregations when I saw the quip, "As goes McDonnell-Douglas, so goes our church." The research into school populations also helped explain why the youth program was suffering a decline.

A review of documents requires finding as much information about the church and community as possible. Agencies such as the *Chamber of Commerce, Census Bureau,* and local *historical societies* can provide additional data. During the search of documents, the key is to be particularly aware of any words and phrases, ideas, phases, or patterns which appear and reappear throughout the local history.

Step 2—Interviews

A second step in gathering data is the interview; both individuals and groups should be questioned. This can take place during the same period as the document search. Interviews can provide information not found in written records, uncover unusual stories, and give deeper meaning to the written records. Sometimes interviews are based on information in the records that needs further clarification; at other times, they are the source of new information.

A good interview needs careful planning, which includes several responsibilities:

1. When *scheduling,* the interviewer should ask for a specific block of time and schedule at the convenience of those being interviewed. The interviewer is like an invited guest, with the interviewee the host.

2. *Have a clear purpose in mind and let the persons know exactly why they are being interviewed.* This means that the interviewer should know what information is important and ask questions designed to discover the data. Questions should be prepared in advance.

3. *Stay on the specific subject and avoid personal matters.* Often the interviewee will offer some information of a personal nature. However, the interviewer asking for information should not seek out the feelings of the interviewee.

4. *Be prepared to conclude the interview at the scheduled time.* As noted above, the interviewer is the guest and should not wear out the welcome.

5. *Try to put the interviewees at ease.* It is always helpful to spend a few minutes with some polite conversation before jumping into the questions.

6. *Listen attentively.* The interviewer should demonstrate good listening skills. Maintain eye contact comfortably, especially when the interviewee is answering. Smile. Give nonverbal cues, such as a nod of agreement or an occasional "yes." It's a good idea to repeat part of an answer for clarity before rushing into the next question. And remember to ask follow-up questions. The interview will be more complete, and the interviewee probably will provide more information if the interviewer listens carefully.

7. *Decide how to preserve the information.* Some interviewers

seek the permission of the interviewee and tape record the conversation. Others take copious notes. Some rely solely on memory and prepare the findings immediately after the interview. The first method is the most accurate; the last, least accurate, but perhaps least intrusive. The interviewer needs to make careful plans and maintain strict control for the sake of accuracy.

At Eastside, I began the interviews with the church staff. I asked several standard questions, both broad and specific, but allowed for enough flexibility to pursue individual interests and ideas. Specific questions, such as "How long have you been on staff?" or "What are your principal duties?" allowed the person to give specific details. Broad questions allowed the staff member to provide more details and personal observations. These questions might include: "What is the most significant part of this ministry?" "How do you see yourself adding to the success of this ministry?" "What is your favorite story about the church?" Both types should be used in order to allow the person to tell you what he or she believes is important and interesting.

In the group interviews, I approached a specific segment of the church: Sunday school teachers, the church council, the clerical staff, officers of the women's group, and so on. The same basic principles applied here: selection of time and place, the preparation of specific questions, and careful listening. A benefit you will receive from the group process is that an idea shared by one member often triggers ideas and causes others to "tailgate" on the same thought. One knows a major theme has been touched when an idea carried by one member is clarified, expanded, or discussed by others in the group. Interviews are a way of discovering more detailed information than the data revealed in written documents. They can generate new information, clarify data that does not make sense, and give a perception of the thinking of the congregation.

One last note—there are several ways of dealing with information generated in the interview. If tape recordings are made, they are usually written out in their entirety. If notes have been taken, they should be reviewed and adapted quickly so that information is not lost. If one is relying strictly on memory, the preparation of notes should be done immediately. Needless to say, this is quite risky because not only might important data be forgotten, but misquoting people is unethical and could lead to unfortunate consequences, along with the fact that uncertainty of exact responses can cloud the issue. I preferred a third way: Working from a careful set of prewritten questions, I allowed enough room on the sheet to write the person's answers. If I wanted to quote someone, I verbally clarified the quote in the person's presence. After the interview, I rewrote my notes and put them safely on a computer file. The written copy was also filed. As the interview process begins, the methods that work best need to be determined.

Also remember that the interviewer is responsible for all necessary materials. If the interview is being recorded, a clean tape, fresh batteries, and *permission to record* are necessary. If the interviewer is taking notes, a spare pen or pencil and plenty of paper should be handy. Finally, the interviewer should stay within the time asked for; the person who granted the time should not be burdened by an interviewer's overextended stay.

Step 3—Observation of Activities

A third step that can take place during the document search and the interviewing process is *observation of the various activities of the congregation.* One should try to observe as many facets of the congregation as possible and, at the same time, be as unnoticeable as possible. Most groups tend to feel uncomfortable about someone watching them as if they were on display, and this might be especially true of those in a position of leadership. A certain amount of fear and anxiety might set in.

The use of a outsider does not eliminate this problem. At Eastside, some groups were easy to observe. For instance, on the Sundays I observed worship, I attended all five services. Since visitors are common, and the congregation numbers between 500 and 800 per service, I was totally unnoticed, even though I was taking notes.

This changed drastically, however, when I attended meetings of smaller groups, especially the normally somewhat "closed" meetings or meetings of specific groups. (Obviously, it was impossible to remain unnoticed at women's meetings.) In these cases, it was necessary to gain permission, and it then became the responsibility of the leaders to explain (or not explain) my presence. Though I only watched in many of these meetings, there were times when I did participate in discussions and activities. The more involved I was permitted to become, the less I was noticed.

As with the document search, the goal of group observation is the discovery of symbols—the recurring themes and ideas. The observer should listen for *stories of past failures and accomplishments, future plans, inside jokes,* and the like. Is the group discussing its plans, its goals? Is it monitoring the results of past efforts? How does this particular group relate to the church as a whole? Is it undertaking any action linked to the announced plans, actions, and goals of the church as a whole? Is its attitude positive or negative about what is happening in other parts of the congregation? Are recurring ideas, themes, words, or phrases heard or read in other places also repeated here? Does this group represent a certain part of the congregation—a "men's" group, a "women's" group, a certain age group? Are there official or unofficial membership requirements? Does it have special traditions of its own? Does the group sense itself as a vital part of the congregation?

In small congregations, it may be possible to observe all existing groups equally over a period of time. In larger congregations, the specific groups observed must be selected carefully. There is a need to determine the variety of groups that are considered in the study. Age, sex, family structures, length of continuous existence, and decision-making authority should be some of the considerations. A representative sample of the entire congregation should be observed.

As with the document search, the goal in group observation is to develop the historical patterns of the congregation. Thus the observer will become attuned to repeated ideas as they are presented. As noted earlier, congregations develop their symbols, the symbols are locked together to produce the symbol systems, and these then become the key components of the congregational story. The document search and observations are two important steps in finding parts of the story. A third step is also helpful—the interview process. Those three steps provide the raw data that will be further researched in Step 4, questionnaires and surveys.

Part B. Processing Information

Step 4—Questionnaires and Surveys

The questionnaire-and-survey step has two purposes. The first is to discover more information about the congregation. Second, questionnaires provide an opportunity to find out whether the ideas produced in the first steps are accurate and carry through in other parts of the congregation.

In preparing the questionnaire for Eastside, I focused primarily on the easily recognized symbols presently known to the majority of the members. Further, I considered several factors, in order to produce a survey that would be as accurate as possible. These factors included establishing the purpose of the questionnaire, targeting the audience(s) to be asked to complete it, eliminating potential biases as much as possible, and choosing a variety of methods for the survey.

First, since there was more interest in testing existing symbols than in developing new ones, I put together a questionnaire which focused on the symbols that were obvious to any careful observer. However, some symbols which had little connection with the symbols discovered were deliberately added to see whether people were simply guessing or were rushing through the questions. For example, a name not associated with the congregation was inserted in a list of commonly known names. In all questions or statements, regular attenders should have been well aware of the common symbols listed.

The only attempt to discover new information through the survey came in two questions asked at the end of the questionnaire. In both, respondents were asked to list any symbols or ideas they might add to those already included.

Second, it was necessary to select the appropriate survey method. It was determined that a variety of methods would be most useful. Selecting from yes/no questions, degrees-of-agreement questions, rank-order questions, and closed or open questions, I selected the degrees-of-agreement and rank-order methods and closed the survey with two open questions.

To determine that the survey was appropriate to the audiences to whom it was to be given and to check for any potential bias, I asked a small number of people drawn from the groups to whom the survey would be administered to do a pretest. Since they were also asked to evaluate the contents for clarity and impartiality, the pretesting resulted in some minor adjustments to the questionnaire.

Finally the target audience was selected. Since Eastside is a large congregation, three types of audiences were chosen. First, an open invitation was issued to the entire congregation. A goal of 100 persons was set, and about half that number actually completed the questionnaire. Second, three Sunday school classes of different ages and interests were asked to participate. Last, a large number of church leaders completed the survey. Altogether, approximately 15 percent of the congregation completed the questionnaire.

Some pitfalls with using surveys and questionnaires should be noted. It is possible to ask "loaded" questions, questions written so that they produce the desired answer. For example, if a question such as, "Are you a faithful supporter of Eastside?" were asked, most people would have responded in an affirmative fashion. Also, one needs to evaluate the data from the standpoint of who is completing the assignment. New or uninvolved members' answers should not be given the same weight as those of leaders or longtime members. Then, there is always a risk that people will give quick answers, not well-thought out or well-reasoned. And some people are not comfortable with their writing skills and will provide only sketchy, incomplete responses. Finally, the tabulations are often done in a haphazard manner; without careful scoring, the results can become quite inaccurate. Care must be taken to use surveys or questionnaires well.

I did two things in my attempt to overcome those problems. First, I asked a friend with expertise in surveys to *check my questions for clarity and objectivity.* After correcting some weak questions, he encouraged me to *do a pretest before the general administration.* Together, we scored and evaluated the pretest survey and the initial results. Then the survey was given and the data tabulated. Again, this authority was consulted to review the results. Though someone in the local congregation may not share this expertise, it is possible in most communities to find someone with questionnaire expertise. Such an expert is often found in a college or university, or a marketing or public-relations firm.

Step 5—Written Report

The final step is *writing the communication story of the congregation*. You should begin with a review of all the materials gathered. At Eastside, I took the results of my findings and compiled a list of all the symbols that appeared in the discovery. Next, they were categorized under the general heading of symbol systems. Common linkages included ministerial staff; lay leadership; men's, women's, and youth activities; missions; special programs; nursery and pre-school programs; building programs; and several others. Finally, the most common thread was searched out—"What do all these ideas have in common?"

It was out of this that the communication story was written. Using the symbols and symbol systems found and keeping the writing in the language I had discovered in the congregation, this document was then given to several key people, selected from those interviewed, for their review and response. They were asked, "Is this your congregation?" After their reviews and comments, the final document was prepared. Needless to say, not everyone agreed with every thought or conclusion; it is impossible to satisfy everyone. The results did give a general story accepted by a majority of the people.

This chapter has offered five key steps for discovering and reporting the communication story of a congregation. The five steps were divided into two sections. In section one, the symbols and symbol systems of the congregation were uncovered, through research of documents, interviews, and observation. Here one identifies those ideas which recur regularly over the entire life of the congregation or at specific periods within its history. The most important ones to consider are those that have a long history and those that are current.

The second section included two steps: the questionnaire or survey and the writing of the communication story. In the study reviewed here, these steps provided a way to check the accuracy of the information found in the first section. New information can be uncovered in both these steps, although it will not be as prevalent.

The primary goal of this process is to determine the symbols, symbol systems, and story of the congregation. It answers the questions, "What are we communicating to ourselves internally and externally to potential members?" Only after the painstaking effort of unearthing what is being disclosed can the actual evaluation begin. Are the symbols used and the story told enabling or disabling? Are some symbols enabling and others disabling? What corrective actions is the congregation willing to take to make the enabling more beneficial and eliminate the disabling? How does it know the difference?

The final two chapters attempt to answer this. They will consider three critical questions:

1. How can a congregation transform its symbols, symbol systems, and communication story to make them more enabling?

2. If this is a new congregation, how can it create enabling realties and symbols that are appealing to its community?

3. How can a church determine to what degree its symbols are enabling or disabling?

VI

Building Enabling Symbols and Communication Story

We pulled into the parking lot of Robbinsdale High School. We stepped out of the car and headed for the doors at the end of the building. On this Saturday evening, my friends Judy and Gordy Bryan had brought me to Robbinsdale for something very special to them. I wasn't quite sure what to expect as we headed inside with a large number of other people.

We moved down the stark halls of the school. The voices of the adults echoed, but they were overpowered by the noises of children. It brought back memories of earlier days, teaching in junior-high and high-school classrooms. Even more, I felt as if it were the late 1950s and early 1960s, and I was back at Lincoln Community High School.

We were on our way to the gymnasium. There was the smell of old tennis shoes and socks. Chairs were set across the floor, and the bleachers were pulled away from the wall on the north side. On the south side stood a platform about six feet high that looked to be about thirty feet square.

People were on the platform setting up musical instruments. They were tuning and checking volumes on electric keyboards, guitars, and a bass; the drummer was working on the tom-toms to get just the right sound. Others were testing microphones. At the front of the platform were a small plexiglass podium and a few chairs.

At the back of the auditorium, people were adjusting lights and working the soundboard for the musicians, and a projectionist was getting some song sheets ready. I was reminded of a high school pep rally.

The people milling around were students looking for a place to sit with their friends. I felt as if I should be on the platform with my trombone. The students were casually dressed in jeans and tee-shirts, shorts and sport shirts. The teachers were in dresses and sport coats.

Gordy and Judy introduced me to a few of their friends as we slowly made our way to some seats in the fourth or fifth row. There were still about five minutes until starting time. Judy said that they would probably run a few minutes late.

It began with a rousing song. The "pep band" and "cheerleaders" were getting us in the mood. Before long, we were all on our feet, singing, clapping, and waving our hands. The sound bounced around the closed, hard-surfaced room. After about thirty minutes, the "coach" stepped to the podium. He was preparing us for "homecoming." He extolled the virtue of our team and closed with a word of encouragement and challenge. I waited for the "football team" to be introduced.

Were we at a pep rally for the local school? Or was this a corporate meeting? Could it be a rally against abortion or pornography? No, it was the Saturday evening worship service of Church of the Open Door in Robbinsdale, Minnesota.

The musicians were the "cheerleaders," and our songs were praises to God. The "coach" was Dave Johnson, pastor of the congregation. The challenge was for a deeper life, or a call to Jesus, based on a text in Matthew's Gospel. And the "team" was composed of Christians gathered for Saturday night worship. Yes, the service was in the Robbinsdale High School gym; Open Door has outgrown two other facilities and the auditorium at Robbinsdale High. The gym is the only room large enough for the crowds. Saturday evening's service is duplicated twice on Sunday morning.

Open Door is an enabled congregation—one of the fastest growing congregations in the nation. It features contemporary, upbeat music and highly excited biblical preaching, often relating the Christian's battles against Satan and his angels. It focuses on the recurring theme, "God, our only hope is you."

The following morning, Sunday, I traveled in the opposite direction from Gordy and Judy's, toward the graceful campus and expansive parking lot of a beautiful new building. I entered the building looking for one of several people I knew. I had attended this church several years earlier and knew that I would see a few familiar faces.

I was fortunate to find a seat in the quickly filling temporary auditorium and found myself behind a friend with whom I had spend many evenings playing Rook. We whispered our greetings and then sat quietly, waiting for the service to begin.

The organist was playing something by either Beethoven or Mozart; I wasn't quite sure which. Suddenly, the sounds of the opening hymn burst forth! The well-dressed people rose to their feet. As the organist began the song for the second time, the congregation sang heartily. From the left, the service participants entered and moved to the platform, followed by the robed choir.

The service was as I remembered. The music was traditional, with choir introits and anthems. A member walked to the pulpit to share her testimony on the "Witness Stand." A trio sang just before Dr. Leith Anderson, pastor of Wooddale Church, stepped up to preach. His was a conversational delivery which led us through the outline printed in the bulletin. That was three-hole punched so that it could be inserted in regular attenders' notebooks of sermon outlines.

Since this was summer, Dr. Anderson was developing a series on contemporary issues. He completed the message; it was followed by a closing hymn, some special comments, the benediction, and the postlude. The service was structured, traditional.

One might assume that this was a disabled congregation. It was not! Wooddale was just a few weeks from completing its nearly $10 million new sanctuary that would seat 2,200 worshipers. Its seven-year-old, thirty-acre campus was already deemed too small. This is another enabled congregation.

Both Open Door and Wooddale must be classed as enabled churches. Both are reaching a large number of people and changing lives with their efforts. This study has contended that congregations are enabled by their symbols and communication story. We have looked at congregations with enabling symbols and stories, and it is now time to focus on the final questions: (1) How have congregations like Wooddale, Church on Brady, and Open Door developed their enabling stories? (2) Can other congregations become enabled? (3) How can a congregation determine whether its story is enabling?

This chapter proposes to answer the first question. We will consider the development of enabling symbols and symbol systems by focusing on two different methods.

Developing Enabling Symbols and Story

There is more than one way to develop an enabling symbol system. Some congregations do so accidentally. They have been fortunate that what has happened to them has been positive. When asked what plan they used, they might suggest that they were simply "led by the Spirit." This is not to diminish the work of the Spirit, but others that make the same claim end up at the other extreme—badly disabled. Wooddale and Open Door used two diverse methods, and though each relied heavily on prayer and the leading of the Spirit, there is more.

Wooddale utilized a very precise strategy; it discovered the symbols of the community and built a congregational symbol system that appealed to the residents. Open Door developed a specialized type of ministry built on key themes and ministries. Those attracted came as a result of finding their needs met by this unique symbol system. Though these two plans are vastly different, much can be learned from each.

Wooddale Method

Step 1—Understand the Congregation

The most basic step in creating enabling symbols is *understanding the congregation's present story.* As outlined in chapter 5, one needs to discover the symbols and symbol systems, and then write the story. In Wooddale's case, this effort centered around a study of its lack of growth. Though it was a large congregation and could have stayed comfortably around the 1,500 mark, it had a strong desire to grow. Its internal study focused on the impact of remaining in the same location, compared to the potential impact of moving to a different community. The study concluded that if Wooddale were to grow into a more vital congregation in years to come, the only alternative was relocation. Though many of the symbols and symbol systems would remain the same, several would need to be changed. The congregation decided that the establishment of a new chapter in the church's story was vital to its growth and development.

The discovery of the congregation's past and present symbols led to the decision to move. The need to discover what new symbols were needed led to the second step.

Step 2—Listen to the Community

The second step required *serious listening*. Just as the congregation listened to its own internal message, it now began to listen for the *new community's symbols*. Many congregations disable themselves because they are out of step with their community's symbols. They have either not heard the symbols or have refused to adapt to them. Wooddale began to study Eden Prairie. The members did much of the work themselves. They conducted house-to-house surveys and asked questions of community leaders. They chose to hire a marketing firm to assist in the analysis. This firm invited groups of people to talk about the needs of the community. They began to create a picture of a typical Eden Prairie family, and from this profile, the symbols began to develop. Three examples will show how Wooddale adjusted their symbols to the symbols of the community.

First, as mentioned before, they found that the name "Baptist" brought to mind a heavy-handed approach to evangelism which would not be welcomed by the community. Thus, the name was changed from Wooddale Baptist Church to Wooddale Church.

Second, the congregation developed a registered trademark: "A place to belong. A place to become." Listening to the needs of the community made the congregation acutely aware that most residents were younger professionals on the way up. They were the "becomers" in their urban setting. They were also looking for something positive on which to build their families. They needed a sense of "belonging."

The motto became a way to say that Wooddale was the place where they could find both.

Third, Wooddale discovered that residents had a high-church background from their Catholic and Lutheran heritage. They had grown up with a traditional worship style, and this led Wooddale to its current building design and worship style.

The building itself is very traditional, including a rather imposing steeple. Like a rural community, where the water tower and the church spire stand above everything else, Wooddale created part of that symbol system. The worship centers on biblical preaching with a Baptist theology, and music of a traditional style focuses on the specially designed pipe organ. Many other symbols could be noted, but these clearly show the carefully designed symbol systems which Wooddale built after listening to its community.

Congregations often disable themselves by paying no attention to community needs. I recently visited with a church member whose congregation had hired a Kentucky native. After four years, he left because he found the ministry "unrewarding" and the members "dissatisfied." The two church leaders who had recommended him were from Kentucky and Tennessee. When they heard his southern accent and southern stories, they identified with him. However, neither the two leaders nor the minister blended into the Southern California culture. They had attempted to build a congregation on Kentucky/Tennessee symbols.

And that is not an isolated example. I once worked with a group of highly educated people who were attempting to start a church in a deeply depressed midwestern town. As leaders, we were attempting to impose our middle-class symbols. Though our intentions were good, we failed to discover and minister through symbols that the community understood.

The enabled congregation knows community symbols.

Much of the success of congregations like Brady and Wood-dale arises from their diligent search for neighborhood symbols. Though outsiders may often become critical of such symbols, they miss the important point of community adaptation. The congregation of Wooddale knows the people of Eden Prairie. The second step is to listen to your community, discover its symbols, and move to build your story harmoniously.

Step 3—Create an Enabling Mission Statement and Matching Goals

After the congregation has completed the first two steps, it should move to the task of *writing (or rewriting, if necessary) the mission statement.* Before a congregation can move forward with enabling symbols, methods, or measures of success, its basic purpose(s) must be stated. Most disabled congregations never put a purpose statement on paper, and as a result, they lack direction. The mission statement sets the stage for symbols that have enabling power. An enabling mission statement should be based on the theology of the congregation and the symbols (needs) found within the congregation and community. Once the work of gathering the symbols of both the congregation and the community has been completed, the difficulty of writing a mission statement should be greatly reduced.

There are many ways to set down the purpose statement. Sometimes the writing is left to a church board and the staff. This was Wooddale's method. Though input from different parts of the congregation was sought, the statement was not presented to the entire congregation until it was complete. In smaller congregations, the members may be invited to participate in every step. In a congregation I once served, this was accomplished through a series of mini-retreats where the desires of the congregation were discussed. Though the elders and staff led the retreats and wrote the statement, the congregation was clearly involved and approved the final outcome with no disagreements or objections.

Though the mission statement often looks simple when completed, the task of writing it is not. Great care must be taken to find the appropriate words; they become powerful symbols that affect the interpretation of the statement. Each and every word should be carefully weighed. The mission statement provides the foundation for the planning process and is the first step in an enabling symbol system.

Once the basic statement is completed, *preparation of long- and short-range goals begins.* These plans should be detailed, so that the congregation has solid, measurable, and reachable intentions. Though the plans may require adjustment as the community and congregation change, they help to develop the enabling symbols. Some symbols and symbol systems might also need adjustment. Fine-tuning is not easy, but it can be done without radical or disruptive changes. Proposed modifications must be carefully evaluated and made only where needed. In some congregations, radical changes could prove disruptive.

An important question about changing symbols and symbol systems exists: Can a congregation change its symbols and symbol systems without affecting its theology? The answer appears to be both Yes and No.

Jesus said, "Neither do men pour new wine into old wineskins. If they do, the skins will burst, the wine will run out and the wineskins will be ruined. No, they pour new wine into new wineskins, and both are preserved" (Matt. 9:17 NIV). It is obvious that Jesus believed that the old wine, or legalism, was no longer flavorful; consequently, it was impossible to put the new wine of the gospel into the old "wineskins." Both were in need of change. However, there are times when the wine of the message is not faulty and only the "carrier" needs to be replaced. The new harvest of grapes deserves a better place to ferment without the necessity of throwing out the fruit in the process.

Further, the question, "What is theology?" must be determined. There are several possible definitions. Do we mean the basic doctrinal statements of a congregation? Do we suggest that even the order of service or type of music selected is theology? It is a tricky question. For this study, I have focused on the basic doctrines of congregations, rather than considering every fine point as a theological issue.

In Wooddale's case, as would be judged about First Christian in Greenville, it appears that the basic theology of the traditions remained very much the same. Though some of the methods of delivering the message changed, the heart of the message remained the same.

The Open Door message did result in a changed theology. Johnson's preaching focused on a shift from a "performance-based" legalism to a "grace-full" message of hope. Attitudes about many issues changed. This switch in theology made people so uncomfortable that several old-timers left. At the same time, new people were drawn in by the new expression of faith. At Open Door, a "new wine" was placed in "new wineskins."

In the end, it is nearly impossible to say that the changing of symbols and symbol systems will not have an impact on theology or that theology will not require new symbols. Any congregation that determines to modify its symbols must look at the impact of both the wine and the wineskins.

Wooddale's method is similar to that used in other places. Saddleback Valley Community Church did not use a marketing firm to discover its community's needs, but uncovered those needs by community surveys and questionnaires in local shopping malls. The methods of discovery are not critical, but the findings are. Such efforts should be done on a regular basis because neighborhoods change. Many congregations remain as old-fashioned as one-room schoolhouses, and they wonder why people are attracted to other places. The reasons are far too obvious.

But the Wooddale model is not the only system that works. The growth of Church of the Open Door has evolved in a totally different way.

Open Door Method

Rather than studying the local community for its symbols and then developing symbols that would appeal to the immediate neighborhood, Open Door has developed symbols and symbol systems in a more generalized way. It looked at the Christian community as a whole and sought to minister to persons who have never been ministered to by churches, or people who have turned away from churches because they found an unaccepting spirit—people discouraged with church in general. Yet they are looking for a faith and assurance that the gospel offers. Open Door has created an enabling ministry which focuses on this particular group of people. I believe that Open Door has followed a specific plan to become an enabling church.

Step 1—Develop Key Symbols for Preaching/Teaching

Though at first glance Open Door's ministry seems somewhat chaotic and unstructured (its people often claim that it is always on the edge of something they cannot identify), it has *clearly defined symbols.*

Several recurring themes are regularly heard in the preaching and teaching of Open Door:

1. *"God, our only hope is you."* This particular symbol system is generated out of some four or five key symbols. Pas-

tor Johnson has consistently developed his sermons around Bible books which emphasize God's grace. Most of his ten years have been spent teaching the books of Galatians, Ephesians, Hebrews, I Corinthians, and Matthew. He has proclaimed that God's grace has replaced humanity's attempts to live according to any legal system. The transformed heart is demonstrated as being more pleasing to God than any outward appearance. He has also portrayed the hypocrisy of the Pharisees in the ministry of Jesus.

2. There has been *a special focus on the need for "brokenness."* Brokenness, in Johnson's teachings, centers on the fact that God works best in the lives of people who are trapped in a pit. Like Alcoholics Anonymous, he has taught that until we are truly down, we will never completely trust God. Along with Jeff Van Vonderen, associate pastor for counseling ministries, Johnson has built a vocabulary around "shame" and "abuse." Open Door suggests that many churches refuse to minister to people who have been broken, shamed, or abused, because they do not "look good." Thus, churches have developed an attitude toward performance and outward appearance much like that of the Pharisees.

3. *"Warfare" against Satan and his hosts* has been another dominate theme. Open Door has taught that many broken people are the victims of the forces of Satan. Their need is for the "deliverance" that is available in the grace of God in Jesus Christ.

4. *Praise is a vital part of worship,* coupled with sound biblical preaching. Praise has defined the type of worship that marks the congregation, so the music is very upbeat. Choruses and Scripture songs are projected on a screen for easy viewing. People generally stand while singing, some clapping in rhythm to the music and raising their hands. Johnson's preaching usually covers a few Bible verses, although he sometimes has focused on a single word. He has spent

nearly a year on Galatians and almost four years on Matthew. His rapid-fire delivery focuses on the content of the text, and on application of the text to the realities of life.

5. Although several themes have been utilized, *the other major focus is the work of the Holy Spirit.* Although Open Door has not taught that any specific charismatic manifestation is the mark of a Christian, Johnson has consistently instructed his people on the availability of all gifts in the church. Open Door encourages its people to use their gifts to the building of the congregation.

Step 2—Develop Staff and Programs Appropriate to the Theology

Open Door has carefully *structured all parts of its program to meet the needs of the people it attempts to address.* This is obvious in two ways. First, the staff has been developed with the purpose of enhancing the teaching goals. Although all staff members are important, two demonstrate this effort most clearly. Jeff Van Vonderen was brought to Open Door to develop a counseling ministry. His books contain the same language heard in Johnson's preaching. He has been on the staff nearly as long as Johnson, and they have worked so closely together that it is nearly impossible to determine who has developed the specific symbols of shame, abuse, and brokenness. Van Vonderen has established a successful professional and lay counseling ministry.

Dan Adler, worship and music minister, is young, energetic, and creative. He has been responsible for the praise part of the Saturday and Sunday services for about five years. Though he does not attempt to build around the themes of Johnson's sermons, he is aware of the symbol systems and develops his praise time accordingly. He remains fully committed to worship that utilizes mostly contemporary, highly energetic music.

All staff members accept the basic truths on which Open Door has built. Persons not committed to these ideals and symbols do not stay.

Programs have been developed around the themes. The most prominent ministries are the counseling and small-group studies led by church members. Although these leaders are not required to have professional training, they are adequately prepared by Van Vonderen and his staff. Currently, there are many different ministries for "shamed" and "abused" people—recovering alcoholics, sexually abused persons, divorced persons, persons abused by parents or spouses, and even those abused by clergy or professional counselors.

Small groups provide times for worship and discussion about the themes developed in preaching. Persons chosen to lead these groups are approved by the staff and elders, and are expected to share the established symbols.

Step 3—Develop a Worship Style to Match
Congregational Symbols

As has been suggested, Open Door's worship has great appeal to the persons committed to this ministry. Since the majority of the 4,000 to 5,000 people who attend Open Door have been "turned off" by the traditional church, this contemporary style has great appeal. They prefer the informality, the upbeat nature, the freedom of expression that flows throughout Open Door. They would agree with those who claim that "churches that still use the pipe organ cannot be growing."

Differences Between the Two Methods

The two methods of building symbol systems possess some similarities. Both methods are audience centered;

they have a definite appeal to people. Both patterns select symbols and symbol systems according to the program being developed. Both have produced very enabled congregations.

But the differences are significant. The major distinction between the two rests in the targeted audience. Wooddale has deliberately built its symbols around the community in which it is located. Open Door has chosen symbols around its view of what people need. Is one superior to the other? Not at all. Both have their place. A key symbol is in the stated mission. Each congregation has a uniquely stated goal, and thus a unique appeal to its predetermined audience.

Another question might be, "Is one more workable than the other?" Here, I would suggest yes. Most congregations are more geared to a particular community, so they would do better by appealing to their immediate neighborhoods. Thus an effort like Wooddale's would prove more useful.

This does not condemn Open Door as not caring for its community; rather, it suggests that its method is more difficult to develop and maintain. Its symbols must possess enough power to carry themselves by word of mouth, and its primary leaders should possess highly charismatic personalities. But either method has validity. The establishment of the key symbol system of the mission and goal of a congregation will generally dictate the remaining symbols. Each congregation must determine its primary target audience.

Wooddale and Open Door could be compared to two different medical practices. Wooddale's symbols and ministries have characteristics similar to those of a general practitioner. Doctor Wooddale moved to Eden Prairie ready to meet the community needs. He is well aware of area specialists and, when confronted with specific problems, does not hesitate to refer to appropriate specialists. Doctor Door is such a specialist. He has declared that he will deal with individuals and families who have been afflicted with diseases of "shame." As a specialist, he must draw patients from the whole Twin Cities area. On occasion, Dr. Wooddale may refer one of his patients to Dr. Door; conversely, Dr. Door may suggest that a patient might be better served by Dr. Wooddale's general practice. Both practices have their place and are successful. And each makes a significant contribution.

Applications to Churches

The application of these ideas to *new* congregations is both simple and obvious. New congregations possess the marked advantage of beginning with a fresh slate. Since they do not yet possess symbols, they can build their symbols and symbol systems from the ground up. They can choose between the two methods or create a completely different model. Though it appears that most would utilize the community-focused method adopted by Wooddale, there are other options.

I have had the privilege of working with a group of college students to establish a congregation in a rapidly developing area in the California desert. Our approach has been similar to the Wooddale pattern. We have used the survey method to discover area symbols. This required much footwork and door knocking, but it has given a clear picture of the area. We also have sought to infiltrate the area by becoming involved in the Neighborhood Watch program. I have volunteered to be both tract coordinator and area coordinator. This allows easy access to many people in the community. And I have begun working with the fire department and the chamber of commerce. Both these organizations provide direct access to community symbols.

We will continue to survey as a means of developing

enabling symbols, and as our method of announcing these symbols to the community. The two initial symbols we have attempted to communicate are "available" and "building." "Available" suggests that we will offer help in times of trouble. "Building" links into the area's rapid development and our desire to grow with the area. New symbols will be added as we learn more.

It is more difficult to apply these ideas to *established* congregations. However, both models have been used by churches in transition. Both of those peaked and then stagnated, yet both eventually transformed themselves into enabled churches. Can all congregations move away from a disabling pattern and become enabling, like Wooddale and Open Door? Probably not. Change will come only when leaders are risk-takers. They will chance people being upset, leaving, criticizing ideas, making personal attacks, questioning motives, challenging authority, and so on. They will understand that the congregation probably will never be the same again. They will know that some people would even prefer to see the church in a disabled condition, if it provides them comfort, rather than be transformed for the sake of becoming enabled. The older the congregation, the greater the probable risk and resistance.

The steps remain clear. There are at least two paths from which to choose. It can be done. However, the move from enabled to disabled is much simpler and less painful than the move from disabled to enabled.

This chapter has demonstrated that change can happen and has shown two clear paths for creating that change. The Wooddale model, the more basic method, maintains that the discovery of neighborhood symbols paves the way for sharing the congregation's message. The Open Door model suggests that the internal message creates the symbols, then seeks an audience to match those symbols.

We have seen that newly established congregations can build symbol systems more easily than older congregations can change theirs. But since it is true that new congregations will create symbol systems either intentionally or unintentionally, a new congregation should be very attentive to what it communicates in its early development.

One more question must be answered: "How can a congregation determine to what degree its symbols and symbol systems are enabling or disabling?" That is the issue addressed in the final chapter.

VII

A Congregation Can Enjoy Enabling Symbols, Symbol Systems, and Communication Story

You are a member of the newly created Outreach Ministry of the New Hope Community Church, a congregation which experienced an average growth of 8 percent annually during its first twelve years. Membership surpassed 1,500, three building campaigns were completed, and weekly attendance expanded to 1,275 four years ago. Since that time, however, attendance has increased only another 40 persons.

Though no serious internal problems appear to have blocked growth—finances have been solid, the building handles all needs easily, the congregation and staff appear mutually satisfied—the nagging problem of slow growth continues. For several months, staff members have studied the problem. They have eliminated external issues that might explain it. The demographics of the area show that population has increased about 22 percent in the past four years. A new elementary school and junior high school have been constructed, and there has been an addition to the high school. A major shopping mall was built two miles from the church property. So what is wrong?

Pastor Bartow and the staff have established a new ministry to further investigate the problem. Each member has agreed to read at least two books before the first meeting. You have read two books on marketing strategies for the church. They are interesting and offer many good suggestions, but do not seem to be talking about you.

After several meetings, the ministry team decides that more help is needed. Pastor Bartow offers the brochures of several consultants who specialize in church growth. He also passes out literature from a new service, Symbolic Communications, Inc., a group that specializes in church-related problems. After reading their brief explanation on symbols and symbol systems, the idea of enabling and disabling symbols leaps from the page.

You think, "What messages have our symbols communicated to the unchurched people around us? If they are aware of our existence, what do they think about us? We have tried programs from church-growth workshops; each has had some positive effect, but growth is still not what had been expected. Maybe it's time to try a different approach."

At the meeting, you suggest that this organization be investigated, and it is agreed that Pastor Bartow will invite SCI to the next Outreach Ministry meeting. You come to the building the following Thursday evening, wondering what this group will offer that you have not heard or read before from church-growth seminars and books.

You are pleasantly surprised to find that the consultants possess ministry experience, as well as advanced communication degrees. For about thirty minutes, they introduce their concept of symbols, symbol systems, and communication story. They talk about the patterns others have used to correlate the symbols of the community and the church. It is a different approach.

You are especially intrigued with the two Minneapolis churches. They are so different from each other, but both are growing significantly. Each had been through a period of stagnation not unlike that of New Hope. You would not argue with the idea that both are enabled congregations according to the definitions offered by the consultants.

But a question keeps coming to you: "How can we tell if our symbols are disabling or enabling? Even if we do all the work, change our symbols significantly, is there any way we can measure the enabling power of the symbols we select?"

The consultants distribute a handout which demonstrates a method they suggest you could use to make that determination. You recognize some of the materials from the business-communication seminar you once attended. It is a simple instrument that has been used in various settings. Though they suggest that it is only as good as the material that is placed on it, they offer several suggestions for making an accurate evaluation. This appears to be a valid way to study the congregation and the community.

How Does a Congregation Determine the Enabling Power of Its Symbols?

Once a congregation has analyzed congregational and community symbols, it must have a means of evaluating the impact of its discoveries. How can it know if change is needed? We will compare the communication stories of Wooddale and Far West to find the answer to the committee member's question.

The format is simple: First, each principle discussed in chapter 1 will be stated and explained. Based on the principle, we will then pose a question which can be rated on a scale. The scale will evaluate the information with examples from the two congregations. Wooddale's position will be located by a W and Far West's with an F. Finally, a brief explanation will be offered to explain why each congregation was located as indicated. Because it addresses the ultimate question, Principle 1 will be considered last.

Evaluating Two Churches on a Scale

Principle 2

An enabled congregation has a clearly defined mission statement and clearly established goals by which to measure its level of accomplishment.

The creation of a mission statement allows a congregation to establish a clear focus from which all other ideas can be directed. From the statement, the congregation can decide whether a program should be implemented. "Does it aid in our mission?" is the key question. Goals can then be established and evaluations completed. Time tables should be built into the goals. Both long- and short-range plans should be developed around the mission statement. The first question about the congregations can be answered immediately.

Question—Do the churches have clear mission
statements and goals?

Yes   No

W									F	
+5	+4	+3	+2	+1	0	−1	−2	−3	−4	−5

One of the significant differences between the Wooddale and Far West congregations arises from this principle. Wooddale has created and seeks to live by its mission and goals. The mission statement has been rewritten on at least one occasion and is the foundation on which all else is built. The structure of the congregation, as well as its motto and programming, are tested by the mission statement. If something does not fall under this basic parameter, it is not used.

Goals and objectives are set forth each year for each part

of the Wooddale ministry, and budgets provide that ministry with the appropriately determined means of support. Though there is a central clearinghouse for major items, the day-to-day operation falls to the ministry team. Programs and budgets are evaluated at the end of the year.

Far West has no mission statement. And although it does set goals occasionally, it has usually failed to establish the means by which their effectiveness can be measured or the ourcome is not accurately measured. Often, new programs are dropped because they are not given time to develop. If there is not immediate success, it is determined that the program has failed and should not continue or be repeated. It is generally suspicious of anything new, since it was "burned" by actions in the past. It prefers to let things go on as they are.

Principle 3

An enabled congregation communicates a wide distribution of power and opportunity.

The idea of power, often associated with corruption and manipulative methods, carries negative overtones for many Christians. Churches have experienced power struggles by less than honest leaders and thus prefer to avoid any indication that any person or group is invested with too much power. However, this definition of power is not a "power *over*" but a "power *to*," which represents a totally different perspective. When placed beside a theology which suggests that every member is a servant who assists the ministry of others, the "power to" do something is highly useful.

The Holy Spirit empowers the church; one of the platforms of the Reformation was the "priesthood of all believers." In recent times, many traditions have emphasized the need for all members to find and develop their spiritual gifts. Passages such as Romans 12 and Ephesians 4 have shown that the work of the church is best accomplished by a majority, rather than by a small fraction. The early church began one of its most rapid expansions when the Jerusalem persecution forced a great many of the believers out of the city and into the countryside (Acts 8), and it was when this large number of people began the task of sharing the gospel that significant growth occurred.

Church-growth leaders suggest that this idea must be repeated. Seminars and classes on developing one's spiritual gifts abound. Studies show that the integration of new members into the church can be accomplished most effectively if they are given the power to work at a meaningful task.

This concept coincides with the communication principle of distributing power and opportunity widely. *Power* does not mean "authority" but "service." This power allows people to *help others,* to *feel that they belong to the whole,* and to *believe that they have something to contribute to the greater good of the church.* Disabled congregations usually are dominated by older, long-term leaders who associate leadership with *control,* not *service.* Such power represents the opposite of this biblical and communication principle. The next graph looks at how widely the two congregations have distributed power and opportunity.

Question—Do the congregations distribute power
and opportunity widely?

Yes   No

	W							F		
+5	+4	+3	+2	+1	0	–1	–2	– 3	– 4	–5

Because of the limited number of people involved, Far West has not expanded its power and opportunity widely.

The willingness to accept new people is limited, so few are eligible for positions, and those who are eligible must be "begged" to serve. Positions are filled as they are required. There is no training ground for replacements and no system in place to determine the skills or desires of the people.

Wooddale is just the opposite. From the time people show an interest in the church, there is an effort to involve them. Talent surveys are given, training programs are in place, and members are encouraged to become actively involved. The "ministry of all believers" is taught as a part of the theology. The small groups into which the congregation is divided assist this part of the ministry because persons are associated quickly with others who know the Wooddale ministries. Leaders of the small groups encourage all to participate.

Principle 4

Enabled congregations maintain open and decentralized communication.

The principle is viewed differently by some church-growth and communication scholars. As I understand the issue, most church-growth material suggests that growth takes place best when there are a limited number of people in decision-making positions, and many decisions must be made without the input of the majority of the congregation. This principle seems to apply especially to the "mega church."

However, communication researchers dispute this. They maintain that the more open the communication across all levels, the greater the level of satisfaction and the more enabled the organization. A recent study of a highly successful manufacturing company found that the company's top executive maintained an open-door policy and often ventured throughout the plant to see how people were doing.

One of the chief complaints among larger congregations is

the lack of communication provided for members and the inability to reach key church leaders. Enabling communication is open and decentralized. Power is shared by accessible people. Determining the success or lack of success about communication will always be difficult. Not only will members have a wide variety of opinions about how much information is needed, they will also claim never to know enough. The key to overcoming the problem rests in a combination of keeping as few secrets as possible and continually opening up lines of communication for all members.

Question—Do the congregations maintain open and decentralized communication?

Yes   No

		W		F						
+5	+4	+3	+2	+1	0	–1	–2	– 3	– 4	– 5

Of all the questions asked, this is probably where the two congregations have the greatest similarity. Wooddale will always have a problem with this because of its size and the tendency for people to want more information than they receive. The majority will almost always expect better communication. Newsletters, bulletins, and public announcements are often missed. Most members will believe that certain people in the congregation know much more than they do.

Far West has a reasonably good communication system because of its size and the closeness that has developed among the remaining members. Often, there is a "rumor chain" that carries the news, and the "rumors" are usually quite accurate. Newer members, however, feel left out of the loop because they are usually the last to know or pick up information from the established patterns. This sense of isolation is part of the reason some do not stay. Only persons on the extreme fringes of the congregation are not tied into the communication patterns, and though they feel left out, they usually are not disturbed because of it. Some prefer not to know.

Principle 5

An enabled congregation uses integrative problem solving.

Integrative problem solving suggests that the persons who raise a question or discover a problem are best qualified to find and implement the solution. Integrative problem solving maintains that most solutions do not need to be made at a "higher level." This is the process which assists enabled organizations; disabled organizations generally require the official decision-makers to reach the appropriate conclusions. Some would question how much the upper-level decision-makers even need to be aware of certain problems.

In disabled congregations, leaders generally insist on making the decisions about even the most ordinary problems: Should a classroom be painted blue or yellow? What time should the seniors meet to go to the museum? Or should they be allowed to go at all? Integrative problem solving allows the appropriate parties to reach their own choices.

Often these issues are controlled by a budgeting process, so that people are forced to ask the appropriate authorities for the monies to do a task. Integrative methods allow people to use their best judgment, if the issue is localized. Thus Sunday school teachers may determine what color to paint their rooms, choir members may decide whether robes are necessary for Sunday evening worship, and so on. Budgeted funds are made available, and the work is done at the level appropriate to the problem.

Further, many congregations have established "task forces"—often called ministries or the like—where certain decisions can be made. Again, the persons chosen for such committees are those who will be most directly affected by their choice. They are enabled because they are the ones who have the most at stake and thus become the most productive problem-solvers.

The next graph locates the positions where Wooddale and Far West fall on the scale in regard to this issue.

Question—Do the congregations use integrative problem solving?

Yes   No

W								F		
+5	+4	+3	+2	+1	0	− 1	− 2	− 3	− 4	− 5

Wooddale encouraged people to make the decisions appropriate to their part of the ministry. Budgets were turned over to the ministries.

Far West had a centralized decision-making process. All congregational matters moved through the church board, and nearly every financial matter was decided by the board. Though some decisions could be made by certain people, most monies were allocated by a single body, and nearly all expenditures were required to be approved in advance. Monies were carefully controlled because "funds were tight." The one exception was the refurbishing committee, controlled by the ruling elder, which had a large budget without any real accountability.

Principle 6

An enabled congregation allows challenge in an atmosphere of trust.

Many congregational leaders do not like to have their decisions or ideas challenged, and rationales are always offered for this protective atmosphere. The most common suggests that leaders should be trusted because they have been elected. They often suggest, "You have chosen us to lead you; either accept our decisions or vote us out. You chose us, now trust us." However, they may hesitate to inform members in advance about their decisions and seldom seek input from the congregation. This nonreciprocal trust factor has a disabling effect on any organization.

Members of the congregation at every level need to trust one another. Often, it is lack of communication that causes mistrust. Perhaps the leadership has not clearly stated why a decision was made, or has failed to make it known that some decisions must be accepted for confidential reasons. However, enabled communication is made in an atmosphere of trust, without manipulation and with sensitivity and openness. Secrecy breeds mistrust. Enabled organizations and congregations build an open, trusting relationship between leaders and members. Disabled congregations work within the confines of secrecy and mistrust. The challenge of any idea is met with some level of hostility or shaming. The following question compares the openness of the two congregations.

Question—Are the congregations free to challenge leadership decisions in an atmosphere of trust?

Yes   No

			W			F				
+5	+4	+3	+2	+1	0	−1	−2	−3	−4	−5

Of all the observations made about the two congregations, this is the most difficult to evaluate. However, it appears that Wooddale's overall attitude of openness allows for challenge more than does Far West's closed attitude. A second problem exists in making this evaluation: How often does the congregation know enough about the official decision-making process, so that it could be prepared to raise a challenge? A great deal of research would be necessary to determine this factor in any congregation.

Principle 7

An enabled congregation provides appropriate rewards and recognition as a means of encouraging performance and responsibility.

Some leaders feel they must accept praise even though someone else may have been responsible for accomplishing a particular task. Consequently, the persons who complete the work are never recognized or thanked appropriately. Churches are no different from other organizations in that respect. A quick and easy way to disable any congregation is to allow people to work without proper recognition. Enabled groups and enabling leaders pay honor to whom honor is due.

Church people may appear to avoid praise because they could be accused of lacking humility. Though they may suggest they do not need recognition, and even seem somewhat embarrassed by it, a vast majority of people need encouragement and the reassurance that they have done a job well. Workers need to be rewarded; this can be done in the form of printed acknowledgments, organized gatherings, plaques, or gifts.

On this last graph, it is noted that both Wooddale and Far West have demonstrated a willingness to recognize their workers.

Question—Do the congregations provide appropriate recognition and reward for their members?

Yes   No

	W	F								
+5	+4	+3	+2	+1	0	−1	−2	−3	−4	−5

One of the great strengths of Wooddale's lay ministry is its regular recognition of persons who accomplish significant tasks both internally and externally. Members are highlighted on a regular basis in the *Wooddale Witness*, the weekly church newsletter. The "FaithStory" platform allows members to present their own testimony before the entire congregation. Banquets and other church programs provide a way to say, "Thank you."

Far West also does a good job in this area. Though it does not provide a forum of sharing as Wooddale does, it often provides gifts for members who have added something significant to the ministry. Generally, such gifts are given to those who are more visible in their service; others, like Sunday school teachers, do not receive such acclaim. An imbalance is noticeable, but rewards and recognition are given.

Principle 1

All organizations possess symbols, symbol systems, and a communication story; all will fall somewhere between the points of enabling or disabling.

As you consider the symbols, symbol systems, and communication story of the congregation you know best, you should look carefully at the messages presented. Though it is difficult, you must be as objective as possible. Are the symbols more positive than negative?

Refer to the nearly thirty items in chapter 1 that describe enabled and disabled congregations. Has your congregation produced more disabling or enabling characteristics? Does it use such terms as "the way it used to be" or "we've never done it that way before"? Or is it ready and willing to accept new symbols by which to identify itself? Then determine where your congregation would fall on the preceding graphs and on the following one. Be as objective as possible, or discuss with others, if you cannot decide alone.

Question—Are the congregation's symbols, symbols systems, and communication story enabling or disabling it?

Yes   No

	W					F				
+5	+4	+3	+2	+1	0	− 1	− 2	− 3	− 4	− 5

Ultimately, I would judge that Wooddale possesses highly enabling symbols, symbol systems, and communucation story, while Far West produces disabling ones.

But that is not the most important issue. It is not what some other congregations have done, but *what is your congregation doing?*

Perhaps you are sitting on the Outreach (Evangelism, Growth, or whatever name is given to it) Ministry of your congregation. You are one of those confronted with the question of growth or nongrowth, and you have the potential to enable your congregation to a greater extent by a study of your symbols, symbol systems, and story.

What is your church communicating to your congregation and community? What do you want to communicate? Can you discover what would help them to see you in a better light? These are important questions, and they require no theology change, only effective communication.

Some Basic Instructions on Interpreting the Findings

It is always difficult to conduct a self-evaluation. The tendency to be either too negative or too positive cannot be overcome easily. As you answer the basic questions above—and any others you feel are important to your congregation—strive for objectivity. A group effort is probably best. A group like the one described at the beginning of the chapter would be appropriate. The following guidelines should be helpful.

1. If all your answers fall to the high range of the "plus" side on the graphs, your congregation should be as vital and growing as Wooddale. It should mean that you are an enabled congregation and are seeing significant advancement, although it is possible for a congregation to be enabled and not see numerical growth. As suggested earlier some enabled congregations simply hold their own or have minimal losses because of their community. It remains a judgment call.

2. If all the answers fall to the high range of the "plus" side, and your congregation is not vital, further evaluation needs to be done. It would suggest either that the symbols and story you have created do not match reality, or that your placements on the scales are faulty. It is probably best if you back up a step or two and strive for more realistic rankings.

3. If the numbers tend toward the neutral range, your congregation probably is in a rut. You have enough growth to sustain the current membership and attendance, but lack the vitality that could move you into the enabled category. Yours is probably not a disabled congregation in danger of dying, but it has not become enabled, either. Two suggestions might be appropriate for the middle-of-the-road congregation: First, look carefully at your evaluations. Have you located yourself on the graph as accurately as possible? Second, look carefully at the symbols of your community. You may have selected very positive symbols for your internal audience, but not for your external audience. Like most of the enabled churches studied, you need to understand the symbols of your community and move to make your symbols and story match them.

4. If your congregation falls on the negative side in nearly every category, it is probably at risk. In such a case, you would do well to go back to the beginning of your exploration and ask, "How can we become an enabled congregation?"

5. Many, if not most, congregations probably will find a mix of both positive and negative. Few congregations do everything well, and few do everything poorly. The logical choice here would be to capitalize on your positive features and strive to overcome the negative factors. Like the congregations in suggestion 4, these congregations will need to refocus their direction.

The Challenge: It's Time to Get to Work!

At the next meeting of your Outreach Ministry committee of New Hope Community Church, Pastor Bartow suggests that you begin with a time of worship and prayer. The group sings some praise choruses, and members share some of their favorite passages of Scripture. You divide into groups of three or four and are given specific matters about which to pray.

On every list, the consistent prayer request is an openness to the leading of the Holy Spirit, as you consider the direction this congregation should be going in the next three years. It is a powerful experience, and after this thirty minutes of preparation, Pastor Bartow challenges the committee to become open to the leading of the Spirit, to be people of prayer, to become risk-takers for the sake of reaching the community more effectively with the gospel of Jesus Christ.

For the next two hours, the discussion focuses on the issues raised by SCI in the previous meeting. The agreement reached suggests that the time has come to look carefully at the symbols of New Hope as they are perceived by the community.

Pastor Bartow says, "Though we believe that we are a friendly, caring congregation, have we conveyed those symbols to our community. Just how do they see us?"

During those hours, a series of decisions are made about the work of the Outreach Ministry. First, you decide that you must come to grips with the symbols of the church and the community. Then you determine which members of the committee will work on what function. Next, you vote to make recommendations to the church council that will enable the congregation to move ahead within the next five years. And finally, you decide to bring in SCI to help the congregation through this process.

The session closes with another time of prayer, focusing on praise and rejoicing. Your prayers are full of thanksgiving and praise for the way God has led you.

A Final Word

I am sure no congregation deliberately chooses to be disabled or wishes to close its doors. Unfortunately, many stand uncomfortably close to that possibility. Church-growth experts have correctly identified several key factors which suggest that some congregations will not survive. More churches than anyone would care to admit are afflicted by terminal illnesses; buildings will continue to be abandoned because congregations have passed the point of no return.

The paradox remains: In the midst of the most incredible time of church-growth research and writing, the majority of American churches grow only slightly. But it is possible for congregations to enjoy a revitalized existence, and there are many ways such changes can be brought about. For instance, since new people are added to congregational rolls again and again as they move from place to place, active evangelism of the unconverted can replace transfers as one key to congregational growth.

The purpose of this book has been to take a look at several enabling congregations from a communication standpoint. It has offered the concepts of "enabled" and "disabled." It has demonstrated that congregations can be enabled by the effective use of symbols, symbol systems, and communication story. It has seen that some congregations have become enabling because they have deliberately set out to reach their communities. They have created strong mission statements and set realistic goals and objectives. They have built their programs to match the needs of the people in their communities. Even churches that cannot explain why they are enabled have created enabling symbols and systems.

The challenge is simple: Your congregation needs to possess and proclaim the gospel message through enabling symbols. Enabling symbols in the church match the symbols of the people and the community. "New wine" is not the need; the "wine" needs new "skins." The skins must be attractive and clearly identified. Then the intoxicating flavor and aroma of the gospel can do its work, enabling congregations to enjoy the fullness of the harvest God desires.

God wants the church to grow. God's Spirit waits to be released. Let it not be quenched because congregations resist the risk of renewal.

The wine of the gospel needs some new skins, and your congregation has the ability to provide them!

I wish you God's blessing.